JUST THE SAME TODAY

CW01095655

Just the Same Today

by

J. OSWALD SANDERS

Formerly General Director, Overseas Missionary Fellowship

OMF BOOKS

| First published | ... | March 1975 |
| Reprinted | ... | May 1979 |

Quotations from the Revised Standard Version and other versions of the Bible are gratefully acknowledged

ISBN 0 85363 105 0

Made in Great Britain

Published by Overseas Missionary Fellowship Belmont, The Vine, Sevenoaks, Kent TN13 3TZ and printed by Stanley L. Hunt (Printers) Ltd., Rushden, Northamptonshire

Contents

Prologue

GOD'S CONSTANCY—OUR CONFIDENCE

'Thou art the same.' Hebrews 1.12.[1]
'Jesus Christ is the same yesterday and today and for ever.' Hebrews 13.8.

The same. Unchanging. Constant. In an unstable and changeful world these two affirmations from the Letter to the Hebrews afford solid ground for our faith. To use an Old Testament figure, amid the swirling currents and raging seas of our times stands Christ, the Rock of Ages, stable and immutable. All that He was in the past He is in the present, and will be in the future.

It is on the constancy of Christ's character that the writer of this Letter bases his appeal to our steadfastness. Throughout history God has always been consistent in His dealings and relationships with His people. He is always the same. His love does not blow hot and cold. We can draw great encouragement from the fact that when He revealed this facet of His nature to failing Israel, He linked His unchanging character to His unfailing mercy. 'I am the Lord, I change not, therefore you, O sons of Jacob, are not consumed.'[2] At first sight it seems a *non sequitur*, but it is gloriously true.

The psalmist expresses the same truth in an equally reassuring manner: 'I will not ... be false to my faithfulness.'[3]

[1] Quotations from Revised Standard Version unless otherwise stated.
[2] Malachi 3.6.   [3] Psalm 89.33.

Both Old and New Testaments bear an unbroken chain of testimony to the immutability and faithfulness of God. He is 'the Father of lights, with whom is no variation or shadow due to change'.[4] He is unchangeable in His holiness, goodness, justice and truth. Even though we prove faithless, 'he remains faithful—for he cannot deny himself'.[5]

It must not be thought, however, that His is the changelessness of inactivity or indolence. He is changeless in the sense that all His activities lead onward to the accomplishment of His eternal purpose. 'Has he said, and will he not do it?'[6]

'Thou art the same.' Such is the thesis of this slim volume. The incidents recounted cover a period of more than a century, during which one missionary society and its members have put the unchanging Christ to the test, and experienced His unfailing faithfulness in cloud and in sunshine. They demonstrate that the God who lived in Hudson Taylor's day is *just the same today.*

The continuing ministry of Him who is our great High Priest is competent to meet the incredible stresses and strains of the space age. Changing conditions and passing years have alike failed to erode His faithfulness.

> *Landmarks along the track that lies behind*
> *Have proved it is Thy custom to be kind—*
> Thou art the same today.
> *Yet with what freshness will Thy tender love*
> *Surprise me on the hidden steps above*
> *As the mists clear away!*
>
> F. *Houghton*[7]

[4] James 1.17.   [5] 2 Timothy 2.13   [6] Numbers 23.19.
[7] This and other verse quoted in these pages are to be found in *Faith Triumphant* by Bishop Frank Houghton, former General Director. OMF BOOKS.

Introduction

SCRIBBLED in pencil on the margin of the original score of one of Frederick Handel's immortal works are the words: *'To God alone the glory!'* He must have known that he had composed a musical masterpiece, but he was careful to ascribe the glory to the One who had endowed him with the appropriate gifts.

In recounting these stories of God's wonderful interventions and provision for His servants under widely differing circumstances, it is our desire to take the same ground. These striking experiences and answers to prayer do not stem from the unusual piety of the missionaries, but from the trustworthiness of the God in whom they placed their confidence. The blessing was theirs, the glory is His.

Over a period of sixty-five years, four books have been published bearing testimony to the faithfulness of God in His dealings, financial and otherwise, with the Mission. The first two, appearing in 1909 and 1933 respectively, dealt with the *China Inland Mission* (CIM) and were written by the Editorial Secretary in the United Kingdom, Marshall Broomhall. The titles were, *Faith and Facts* and *Our Seal.* The second two, both written by Phyllis Thompson, were concerned with the *Overseas Missionary Fellowship* (OMF) the heir to the China Inland Mission. They carried the titles, *Proving God* and *Our Resources*, the last named being written in 1965 to commemorate the Centenary of the Mission.

Why a fifth book? We read in ancient times 'there arose a new king over Egypt, who did not know Joseph'.[1] The signs and wonders in which God had displayed His power to deliver and His care for His people in impossible situations were unknown to that generation, with tragic results to both Egypt and Israel.

The leaders of the OMF have felt that it would be to God's glory and to the enrichment of His Church if the remarkable story of the Mission were brought up to date. Christians of this generation can thus see that God is just the same today, and be encouraged to emulate the faith of their contemporaries. Faith is contagious.

In compiling this record, I have drawn freely on the volumes previously mentioned, and acknowledge this general indebtedness here, rather than breaking the thread of the story with individual acknowledgements. The incidents drawn from the past serve to demonstrate the wonder of the same Lord's provision in our day against the background of His faithfulness yesterday. The stories of faith's quest and conquest illustrate the continuing relevance of the principles on which the China Inland Mission was established over a century ago.

In order that readers may be able to follow intelligently the different names used for the Mission in the book, a brief history of the Mission is given in the Appendix.

[1] Exodus 1.8

For the Birds

'Look at the birds of the air: they neither sow nor reap nor gather into barns, and yet your heavenly Father feeds them. *Are you not of more value than they?'*[1]

The earliest statement of the financial policy of the China Inland Mission was couched in simple yet pregnant words, words which in the main express the continuing policy of the Overseas Missionary Fellowship.

'The needs of the work are laid before God in prayer, no personal solicitations or collections being authorised ... Their faith must be in God, their expectation from Him. The funds might fail, the Mission cease to exist but if they put their trust in Him, He *will not fail or disappoint them.'*

On being informed of this financial policy of the OMF the response of one modern missionary aspirant was 'Oh, that is for the birds!' The obvious implication of this cynical appraisal was that in our sophisticated age such a concept was altogether too ethereal and impractical for thinking people. But is it?

The original constitution of the CIM was drawn up with the conviction that its leaders and members were not dealing with a remote and unconcerned God, but One who always responds to the sometimes trembling

[1] Matthew 6.26.

faith of His children; a God who without fail and at the right time will meet the needs of His children, whatever they might be.

Going into debt whether as a Mission or as individual members, then as now, has been regarded as inconsistent with the principle of complete dependence upon God. The presumption implicit in Philippians 4.19 is that if there is a genuine need, He will supply it; if He does not supply, then it is not a genuine need.

> *Since on His promise I rely*
> *That God will all my need supply,*
> *The inference is clear indeed—*
> *What God withholds I do not need.*
> *So, with His goodness satisfied,*
> *I rest, nor ask for aught beside.*
> *F. Houghton*

Since God is sovereign, can He not guide and educate His servants as well by what He withholds as by what He bestows?

God is bound by His Word to answer the prayer of faith for anything that is in the interests of His work and for the ultimate benefit of His workers, and the experience of the Mission over more than a century has proved a policy based on this premise to be neither ethereal nor impractical. The receipt of the sum of US$2,700,000 without solicitation during the last financial year is solid and satisfying evidence that it is still safe to trust God.

One of the severest tests which the Mission and its financial policy ever faced, occurred in 1950–1952 when the Communist take-over of China compelled the withdrawal of the 627 missionaries and their 200 children scattered all over that vast land. This complex operation involved no less a sum than £113,000, towards which there was only £1,500 in the treasury at the time. If ever there was an opportunity to demonstrate the validity of the Mission's traditional policy, this was it.

No appeal was made, except in prayer, but all over the world interested friends laid hold on God. Nor was their importunate prayer denied. When the last missionary emerged from China, the Mission Treasurer was able to report that not one missionary had been delayed for one day, either in China or on the way to their homeland, solely through lack of funds. Every obligation had been promptly met. There had been other hindering factors but none attributable to God's failure to supply the required finance at the right time.

But this was not all. While this protracted withdrawal was in progress, God had been guiding the Mission leaders to commence new work in a number of countries in East Asia, and to redeploy as many of the missionaries as elected to serve in the newly opened fields. So, while weary and much-tested missionaries were slowly emerging from Communist China, others were commencing pioneer work in areas which were largely, and sometimes entirely, unreached with the gospel.

To God's glory it can be stated that sufficient funds were received to maintain the costly two-way movement and to establish the new work to which God had called.

The writer has no intention of conveying the impression that the stories which follow are every-day occurrences. It will be apparent to the reader that they are highlights in the normal life of the missionary. They should not obscure the less spectacular though equally remarkable miracle of daily supply through normal channels. The constant provision for the requirements of a mission family of about 1,500 active members, retired members and children without recourse to solicitation, is no ordinary occurrence.

Today the Mission's annual budget nears the £1,500,000 (or US$3,000,000) mark, so, in addition to the occasional large gifts, there is plenty of room for the help of thousands of small donations. Is not God's faithfulness as clearly demonstrated in such giving as in His more spectacular emergency interventions?

When we read of Abraham's encounters with God, we are inclined to forget that these were rare highlights in his experience. Between these peak experiences lay the monotonous years of ordinary living. Twenty-five years elapsed between God's promise of a son and its fulfilment. God was perhaps more glorified in the long drawn out test of Abraham's faith than in his crisis experiences.

It would be less than ingenuous to say that there have not been those within the membership of the OMF who have been critical of the Mission's financial policy, and have advocated the adoption of another. It must be admitted, too, that they marshalled some cogent reasons for a change. But although the subject has been reviewed on more than one occasion and the views of all members canvassed, the consensus of opinion remains over-whelmingly in favour of maintaining the current financial basis.

Over the century of the Mission's history, this policy has been tested in the fires of martyrdom, war, revolu-tion, financial collapse, incredible galloping inflation and Communism. Today the OMF remains committed to it. It is their testimony that their trust has not been betrayed.

There have been agonising crises and desperate shortages. Individual missionaries have been tested almost beyond the limit. There has been failure in mission administration. Oftentimes the testing has continued to the last possible moment. But in the nick of time God's answer has come.

The normal experience has been that prayers are answered and funds come in. But in those cases where there has been delay or denial the outcome has usually brought more blessing than would exemption from the trial.

In this record there is neither desire nor intention of denigrating the policies of any sister mission. It is not claimed that this is the only Biblically-based financial policy, or that it is superior to any other. It may well be, as some have claimed, that other policies demand a higher degree of personal as opposed to corporate faith. All we would say is that this is the policy God led the Founder of the CIM to adopt, and succeeding genera-tions of missionaries have seen no compelling reason to abandon it in favour of another.

The Mission has indeed proved it to be a policy '*for the birds*'! The logic of our Lord was that if our Father cares sufficiently to provide for the daily needs of the birds, as He does, how much more will He provide for His trustful children. 'Your heavenly Father feeds them, and how much more precious you are than they.'[2]

But this assurance of divine provision does not carry with it the presumption of exemption from trouble and testing. It does n t dispense with the necessity for the exercise of faith. The lesson to be mastered is that although we may experience trial and misfortune, we may and should always be free from faithless worry and care.

[2] Matthew 6.26 (paraphrase).

The School of Faith

GOD places faith very high in His scale of spiritual values. Indeed, 'without faith it is *impossible* to please him.'[1] There is no acceptable substitute.

The Apostle John shared with his Lord the conviction that the cultivation of faith is one of the most important factors in God's dealings with His people. He made this clear when he stated his purpose in penning the Fourth Gospel :

'Now Jesus did many other signs . . . which are not written in this book; but these are written that you may believe . . .'[2]

Jesus explained in somewhat similar words the hidden purpose behind His delay in hastening to the side of His stricken friends, Martha and Mary, when He heard of Lazarus' serious illness : 'for your sake I am glad that I was not there, *so that you* may believe.'[3]

A somewhat similar purpose lies behind the writing of this book. The sharing of the intimate experiences that follow is first, to demonstrate God's faithfulness to His plighted word, and second, to encourage the reader to put Him to the test. For this there is Scriptural warrant : 'Bring the full tithes into the storehouse, that there may be food in my house; and thereby put me to the test, says the Lord of hosts !'[4]

George Müller was a close friend of Hudson Taylor and throughout his long life was a generous donor to the

[1] Hebrews 11.6.   [2] John 20.30, 31.   [3] John 11.15.
[4] Malachi 3.10.

China Inland Mission. In referring to his celebrated Orphan Homes on one occasion he said, '*Their supreme object is to prove God's faithfulness*, and the perfect safety of trusting solely to His promises . . . to lead those who are weak in the faith to see that there is reality in dealing with God alone.'

It sometimes appears as though God deliberately allows acute crises to develop, and desperate, even impossible, situations to arise, in order that His servants might have fresh and unmistakable evidences of His activity on their behalf. Divine love permits severe testing, not for its own sake, but because in this crucible alone can faith be purified and strengthened.

In the light of this fact it will be readily understood that Hudson Taylor who, like Abraham, had been marked out by God to become a pioneer of faith, should early in life experience testing in the School of Faith. The moving story of his initiation into the life of faith when only sixteen years of age is recounted in *The Biography of James Hudson Taylor*. This experience profoundly influenced him in after life, and laid the foundation of trust in God that later found fuller expression in the China Inland Mission.

From the inception of the Mission in 1865 until today, restful confidence in the utter trustworthiness of God and of His promises has been our underlying philosophy.

Early in his missionary career, while engaged in studying a familiar Scripture passage, Hudson Taylor made a transforming discovery. He found that the verse, 'Have faith in God'[5] could be translated with equal propriety, '*Have the faith of God*',[6] or '*Hold, reckon on, God's faithfulness*'.[7]

[5] Mark 11.22.   [6] AV margin.
[7] Hudson Taylor's paraphrase.

This discovery held alluring possibilities for him. 'The man who holds God's faithfulness,' he wrote, 'will dare ιο obey Him, however impolitic it may appear. Holding His faithfulness, we may count on grace for work, on pecuniary aid, and on ultimate success.' In spite of devastating reverses, shattered health and multiplied trials, he never went back on that conviction.

This bracing and stimulating truth inevitably became a dominant factor in the life of the young mission. Its literature is studded with references to the faithfulness of God, and exhortations to hold it fast.

In the following selections from the writings of the Founder and subsequent Mission leaders, will be found the seed-bed of its original and continuing financial policy.

'There is a living God. He has spoken in the Bible. He means what He says, and will do all that He has promised.'

'God's character is the Mission's guarantee, for it is built upon His Word. God has pledged Himself by His promises, and confirmed the promises by an oath.'

'From the beginning the Mission has staked its very existence on the faithfulness of God. His promises have been taken at their face value. They have been put to every conceivable test. They have been proved in many painful emergencies. They have passed triumphantly through the crucible of war, and they have never failed. God's Word has been found to be a rock that cannot move.'

'There is no tension in trust. As the habit of trusting God is formed, strain ceases. Trust precludes anxiety and worry. The presence of anxious care betokens the absence of confident trust.'

'There is no such thing as faith without trust. Trust is effortless confidence, based on the character of the One in whom it is reposed. True faith will always issue in full trust.'

'Faith feeds on the pledged Word of God, and flourishes in the atmosphere of His presence.'

'If anyone does not believe that God speaks the truth, it would be better for him not to go to China to propagate the faith. Depend upon it, *God's work done in God's way will never lack God's supplies.*'

'Want of trust is at the root of almost all our sins and all our weaknesses. And how shall we escape from it but by looking to Him and observing His faithfulness?'

'A step of faith always involves a calculated risk. It is not blind credulity, but calm confidence. The heroes of faith had their portraits hung in God's Hall of Fame because they were willing to stake everything on His faithfulness. Had there been no element of risk in their exploits, faith would not have been necessary.'

'The Lord is always faithful. He tries the faith of His people, or rather their faithlessness. People say, "Lord, increase our faith".[8] Did not the Lord rebuke the disciples for that prayer? He said in effect, "You do not want a great faith, but faith in a great God, which expects Him to keep His own word".'

'How many estimate their difficulties in the light of

[8] Luke 17.5 AV.

their own resources, and thus attempt little, and often fail in the little they attempt!'

'My experience proves that to *those who do not trust Him wholly*, still He is wholly true. He does not break His Word, nor cast off His children in their weakness and trial. No! He is always gracious and tender. "If we believe not, He abides faithful. He cannot deny Himself." '[9]

'Faith is reliance on the trustworthiness of those with whom we transact business. Our faith is the recognition of God's faithfulness. It is so blessed to leave our faith out of account, and to be so occupied with God's faithfulness that we cannot raise any question whatsoever.'

It would be false to experience if it were not acknowledged that, as well as the certainties of faith, there are the perplexities of faith. It is the mood of the pragmatic youth of today to distrust a record that is 'all cheers and no groans', as someone put it. They rightly maintain that life is just not like that. There is agony as well as ecstasy. The history of the Mission has not been a constant pageant of triumph, an unbroken succession of miracles of divine intervention with no experiences of failure. But it is our testimony that through it all, God has proved unfailingly faithful.

Nor has the Mission been exempt from experiences that have tested faith to the limit. It is not God's method to answer every question of His querulous children or to explain every ambiguous action. Were He to do so, where would be the necessity for faith? It is in just such circumstances that faith achieves its finest triumphs. Faith takes its highest flight in the darkness.

[9] 2 Timothy 2.13 cf. AV.

The patriarch Job reached the highest pinnacle in his life and brought the greatest glory to God when he was utterly mystified at His dealings with him, yet steadfastly refused to cast away his confidence. 'Though he slay me, yet will I trust in him.'[10]

How mysterious, how inexplicable in human terms was God's apparent silence during the Boxer Rebellion of 1900 when fifty-eight CIM missionaries and twenty-two children, as well as numberless Chinese Christians, became martyrs for their faith! There was no glib answer to the appalling tragedy. As blow upon blow fell upon the Mission leaders and membership, they could only say in trembling faith, 'Even so, Father: for so it seemed good in thy sight',[11] and leave the explanation until they reached the Better Land.

Stories are told in this book of almost miraculous deliverances of missionaries. One of the early Home Directors of the CIM, in Britain, Dr. J. Stuart Holden, was booked to sail to the United States on the ill-fated "Titanic". At the last moment God intervened, and he cancelled his berth.

But how explain the tragic death in a 'Comet' crash of Mr. Fred Mitchell, when he was Home Director for Great Britain? The author was with him in the Singapore Mission Home when it was suggested to him that he should change the plane booking he held, for a flight on the 'Comet'. 'If you do, you will have breakfast with your wife a day earlier', said one of the men. The change was made.

Hard-pressed faith would ask, Why did God allow His child to change his flight? But faith had its triumph when his widow was able to accept without explanation the Master's words to Peter, 'What I am doing you do

[10] Job 13.15 AV.   [11] Matthew 11.26 AV.

not know now, *but afterward you will understand*.[12]
Part of the divine purpose has already been discerned in
the blessing that has come from the story of his fragrant
life entitled, *Climbing on Track.*

> *We do not ask Thee to explain*
>   *Why Thou has acted thus, nor how*
> *Such seeming loss is turned to gain,*
>   *Eternal gain—but even now,*
> *Acknowledging that all Thy ways*
>   *Are right, we offer Thee our praise.*
> *F. Houghton*

[12] John 13.7.

'He Gives His Angels Charge'

The danger that His love allows
Is safer than our fears may know;
The peril that His care permits
Is our defence where'er we go.

In 1947 while I was travelling on horseback in central China with Mr. Fred Mitchell, we came to a spot that was notorious as a robber hide-out. The missionary accompanying us was keeping a sharp look-out. Suddenly we came upon a body lying beside the path. The victim was obviously not long dead. The brigands had been at work.

A few days later I received a letter from my wife, asking whether we had been in any danger on a date and at a time she named. On that particular night she had been suddenly awakened with the strong impression that I was in danger. She rose and prayed until the burden lifted and peace returned.

On consulting my diary, I discovered that this midnight prayer synchronised with the time we were passing through that robber-infested area. God heard and answered the prayer for the safety of His servants.

Travel in some eastern lands is often a precarious and nerve-wracking experience. Normal standards of safety are honoured more in the breach than the observance. Under these conditions, the prayer of the missionary for safety in travel soon loses its formality and becomes a heart-felt plea. The aeroplane has added a new dimension to the problem. But we have the comforting assurance that God's faithfulness 'reaches to the clouds' too!

It was late in 1944, when the Japanese were pressing towards Chungking. Instructions were received that the little primary school in Kiating, which had been opened for the children of missionaries in Free China, was to be evacuated to India.

An American lorry arrived at the Mission compound to collect twenty-five children and two lady missionaries who were to accompany them, and convey them to the airfield. They spent Christmas day there, waiting for the plane that was to take them to Kunming and thence across the mountains of the Salween divide and Burma to India.

Hearty helpings of turkey and Christmas pudding served on metal trays by generous GIs did much to maintain tradition, and in spite of the unusual circumstances, the festivity usually connected with the season was by no means lacking. It was not until late afternoon that the plane actually arrived and the children, hugging dolls or toy trains or stamp albums, clambered excitedly up the gangway for their first aeroplane trip.

'We haven't got parachutes for the children, so we can't give them any,' observed a member of the crew to one of the women. 'You wouldn't jump without the children, so it's no use giving them to you. And we wouldn't jump without you—so I guess we won't take any parachutes this trip.'

They got settled at last. The door was shut. The engine started to hum. Then, suddenly, it was switched off. Something was wrong with the pressure gauge. It must be repaired before they could start. Then the pilot said casually, 'Might as well load on some more fuel while we are waiting'. No, he knew they didn't need it, but they might as well load it now—it would save time when preparing for the next flight.

The pressure gauge was repaired, the fuel loaded, and eventually the plane took off as darkness was falling. It usually took two hours to fly to Kunming, but two hours found them still flying high.

'When do we reach Kunming?' one of the missionaries asked a member of the crew.

'Oh, in about an hour or so,' he replied vaguely. What he did not tell her was that an air-raid warning in Kunming had resulted in a black-out and the pilot had lost his bearings. They were flying around in the dark, over unknown, mountainous territory, afraid to come down because of the low hills and unable to distinguish any familiar landmark. And of course the fuel was running out.

They flew on and on. Oxygen was handed round, but soon that was all used up, and some of the children became sick, gasping for breath. Still the pilot could not get his bearings. The fuel tank would run dry in another half hour and then . . .

But suddenly there were twinkling lights discerned below. The pilot, straining his eyes, recognised them. They were over an airfield! A place to land, free of mountain peaks or paddy-fields, at last!

'Let me get out and kiss *terra firma*!' ejaculated one of the crew as he came out of the cabin. 'Never again!' For he knew what the missionaries learned only later— that had they remained in the air *for ten more minutes*, the fuel would have run right out.

Just ten more minutes! Had it not been for that

extra load, added so casually to fill in the time, the plane would have crashed an hour before!

But there are still many tribal areas in Asia where there are no airstrips, and unromantic foot-slogging is the only way for pioneer missionaries to reach those to whom they wish to bring the gospel.

Doris Pack was one OMF missionary who had perforce to adopt this mode of travel to reach the Mangyan tribespeople in the Philippines. Mountain tracks are rough and slippery, and bamboo bridges both treacherous and dangerous. On one such journey Doris suffered a near-fatal fall. Concerning it she wrote in her cheery style:

'I am convalescing again! However I can only thank the Lord I am able to convalesce, for I took quite a tumble on the trail a few weeks ago and nearly scalped myself. I slipped on a ledge by a waterfall and landed on the rocks below, gashing my forehead and scalp along the way. My "fatal beauty" has been somewhat marred and I will have some real battle-scars to display; but my head is a hard nut to crack. Fortunately I did not suffer any concussion or fractures.

'After a week of good care by fellow-missionaries in Pinamalayan, and daily visits from the Filipina doctor there who stitched me up, I was able to proceed to Manila for X-rays and now I am just fine again. My doctor friend said, "I guess your work here isn't finished yet".

'As the Lord has graciously spared my life, I want all the more to give myself to Him to accomplish the work He has for me here.'

Two missionaries in Central Thailand were returning

by bicycle from visiting a leprosy patient when a gang of armed men waylaid them. They took their bicycles and watches, and then led them over the fields to the wooded part at the foot of the low hills.

Understandably, the girls were apprehensive of what might lie ahead. But God's angels restrained the men. And better than that, 'we both had opportunities to tell them of the Lord, and that He was watching over us and would care for us. It was as though a canopy of the Lord's protection was over us.'

We should not regard prayer for the protection of missionaries from the hands of wicked men or from natural disaster as a mere matter of form. It is a subject that should have a regular place in missionary prayer meetings, for it is an ever-present reality in our disordered world.

Dick and Rosemary Dowsett felt the need for such prayer in a series of incidents that befell them in the Philippines.

'In November 1970 a terrible typhoon over Manila flattened buildings and crops,' Rosemary wrote, 'but our only damage was a broken window.

'In December we spent three hours barricaded inside a cinema, while a street battle, bombs, shooting and all, raged outside between rioting students and the police.

'Several times we have been caught in violent demonstrations, where to be large and white is to be unsafely conspicuous.

'Dick has been threatened with his life by three robbers on a bus. A thief tried to break my watch off my wrist as I walked along the road.

'In January 1971 a tremendous fire destroyed many streets of houses—and stopped just the other side of

UST from us.[1] All this within three months. *It is no idle request when we ask you to pray for our safety.'*

Theirs is by no means an isolated case. When the bus on which Dr. and Mrs. Gordon Gray were travelling in South Thailand was held up, and all the passengers robbed, the man sitting next to Gordon was shot and killed.

The Robin Talbots tell of visiting Méo refugee camps and an army 'Fortress' near Cawca in North Thailand, where they were met with a warm welcome. On another occasion, despite the warmth of their previous welcome, they had no peace about visiting the 'Fortress'. Later they drove past it again and found tyre marks and spare cartridges littering the road. An ambush had taken place, and their providential delay to procure oil and petrol had saved them from possible death.

The young missionary finds his early inability to speak the language of the people a very frustrating limitation, but there are times when it can hold even more sinister implications.

'Ever tried explaining to someone that your stove is on fire—when you don't know the word for stove?'

That was the predicament in which Mary Jane Faircloth found herself one Friday afternoon in early 1973. She had started to turn off her kerosene stove, when the left-hand burner did a side-flip. Fire shot upwards towards the ceiling and down into the reserve tank.

'I quickly realised that this was one fire that wasn't going to burn itself out. And I remembered that you don't use water on any kind of oil flame. Then, too, I

[1] University of Santo Tomas.

recalled someone saying, "This type of stove sometimes explodes if it catches fire!"

'Since I was alone at the time, I decided to get some instant practice in the use of the Indonesian language! The first person I encountered was a man eating at the food stall next door. And that's when I couldn't think of *kompor*, the Indonesian word for stove. But I thought I had got around that until he said, 'Yes, glad to help you, miss, but is it OK if I finish eating first?'

'So what happened next? Did the Lord miraculously bring to my mind the word *kompor*? No, as a matter of fact He didn't. But I suddenly remembered the word *berbahaya*, Indonesian for "dangerous". And that got the message through to the man a lot faster than the word *kompor* would have done.'

Yvonne Cooke, too, has her fire story.

'We were abruptly awakened about 2.30 a.m. A cushion-making factory situated about fifty yards down the road from us, on the opposite side, had caught fire.

'Enormous flames were leaping high in the sky and were speeding in our direction. When I saw how quickly and easily they began to lick the roof of the wooden house next to it, I realised how serious it could be for us.

'We dressed, grabbed our passports, packed some of our clothing and valuables and carried them to a house some distance away where some of our language students live.

'By the time we returned, a fire engine had arrived and was pumping the water out of the pond at the back of our house. There was no other water available, so our dirty old pond saved the day! People around feel that but for this, the fire could have devastated the whole area. Only a few houses away from where the fire stopped, are three wooden houses where other OMF workers live.'

In the midst of all this excitement, Yvonne recalled the Daily Light portion which she had read just before going to sleep: 'God is my defence ... The Lord is round about His people.' She felt compelled to confess, however, 'I had the same sort of feelings as I've had on rough boat crossings.'

> *How can we fear?*
> *For love delighteth ever*
> *To meet our need.*

It was the devil who quoted the Scripture, 'He will give his angels charge over you'.[2] But the fact that he quoted it does not vitiate its truth. The staff of the OMF Hospital at Saiburi, South Thailand, have experienced such angelic protection. Dr. Clarence Yand, the Hospital Superintendent, shares with us some of the unenviable experiences in 1971.

'For many years the staff of the hospital have lived and carried on their work cheek by jowl with some of the terrorist elements that infest South Thailand. These groups had hitherto refrained from hindering the work and ministry of the hospital, although they had often made their presence and influence felt.

'Shortly after midnight on November 10th, we were suddenly awakened by the sound of automatic weapons firing into the hospital compound. The police were called and the firing soon stopped. A search of the compound revealed that two staff houses had been hit, but there was no further sign of the gunmen.

'The numerous bullet holes and wood splinters left us in no doubt as to their intentions, however. There were

[2] Luke 4.10.

a number of miraculous escapes, with bullets hitting just a fraction of an inch away from some of the sleeping girls. One Christian Thai nurse aide, whose pillow was struck, had left only a short time before to go on duty. The only missionary whose bedroom was struck was also on duty in the hospital. How conscious we were of the Lord's watchful care over us !

'Two days later, the mail carried a letter from the terrorists threatening to attack the hospital again and to destroy it, unless a substantial amount was paid to further their cause. Local authorities informed the Governor of Pattani Province of these threats and he took immediate steps to secure the hospital with a police guard.

'After consultation with our national staff, particularly the Christian men, and prominent local citizens, we felt we should continue to operate the hospital as before. Our national staff responded to the emergency with great loyalty and a growing sense of responsibility. Although they were all given ample opportunity to leave if they wished, the fact remains that not one of them has left us in the face of terrorist threats.

'During this period of tension and uncertainty, we missionaries have been privileged to share and have fellowship with our national colleagues in a new way. Within one week three people came to the Lord, two patients and a relative, one of them a young Malay man. Together we are continuing the work at Saiburi with a new sense of urgency.

'We believe that God is leading us into a new era of greater witness, accomplishment and usefulness than ever before. While we have no strength or safe defence in the face of such an enemy, we are sure of God's strength and His amazing ability to turn evil around to bring honour to His name, and to further rather than hinder the progress of His gospel.'[3]

'Our God turned the curse into a blessing.'[4]

Was there ever a peril that found Thee unprepared,
A need of flesh or spirit that Thou didst not foresee?
When darkness overwhelmed me, how should I have fared
If the light and darkness were not alike to Thee?

F. Houghton

[3] The story of how Minka Hanskamp and Margaret Morgan were held as hostages will be told elsewhere.

[4] Nehemiah 13.2.

A Divine Timekeeper

THERE was one crucial moment when the diverse paths of the Ethiopian Chancellor of the Exchequer and Philip the evangelist would intersect. Had Philip been one minute late, the Ethiopian would have returned home with Isaiah's enigmatic passage unexplained. Had Philip stopped to argue with the angelic messenger about the advisability of leaving the flourishing revival in Samaria for a desert rendezvous, the Ethiopian Empire would have been denied the knowledge of the gospel. But God had the timing in His competent hands.

The sensitive observer can discern a similar meticulous timing in the detailed outworking of God's missionary programme. Some prayers must be answered by a certain time, or not at all, and the miracles of divine timing are just as real miracles as was the feeding of the five thousand. The stories that follow are examples of the accurate timing of a God who is never too late.

For more than ten years after Dr. A. J. Broomhall received a clear call from the Lord to go to the Independent Nosu in West China, he searched for any available information about the formidable Nosu people, but with very limited success. When he and his wife returned to China from furlough in 1946, it was to go at last to 'Nosuland'. Already they had had five years of Chinese language study and medical experience, and six months among subjugated Nosu at Kiehkow in Kweichow Province. But their knowledge of what to expect in the distant Independent Nosu area was minimal.

For months Dr. Broomhall had been trying to track down a Chinese anthropologist who had visited Nosuland and had written some papers on cultural topics. The British Council and the consular service had been unable to discover his whereabouts.

When the Broomhalls arrived in Shanghai, Bishop Houghton, then General Director of CIM, put before them with many apologies a proposition to pray about. 'He assured us that we were under no obligation to act on it, seeing that he had promised that we could go without delay to Nosuland.'

'Rupert Clarke', he said, 'is tired and overdue for furlough, but there is no doctor to relieve him at the Borden Memorial Hospital in Lanchow. Will you consider going there before proceeding to Nosuland? We will send another doctor to replace you as soon as we can.'

As soon as they prayed about it, they knew they should comply, and told Bishop Houghton so. A day or two later they boarded a plane for Lanchow, a thousand miles distant from Nosuland.

They had not been airborne for very long before Dr. Broomhall noticed a large oil leak from the starboard engine of the DC3 in which they were flying and knew they were in for trouble. On they flew until at last they landed at an airfield outside a large town. The whole of the underside of the plane was black with oil, and the engine was wrecked.

'Find yourselves somewhere to live,' the pilots said, 'and enquire tomorrow whether arrangements have been made for you to continue your journey.'

They picked up their handbags and, carrying their two small children, started walking into the town to look for lodgings. Suddenly, to their amazement, they saw coming along the pavement a Methodist missionary couple who had been on their ship as far as Hong Kong.

'What are *you* doing here?' they said simultaneously. When they heard of the predicament, the Methodists invited the travellers to their home. While the children were being fed and put to bed, the missionary said, 'Come over to the university where I am teaching, and meet some of my colleagues'.

The first colleague to walk into the common-room was the professor whom Dr. Broomhall had been seeking with so many prayers for so long. They spent the rest of the evening together, and the next day continued the journey to Lanchow. In their luggage was a sheaf of monographs and a book by the professor, which made it possible for them to approach the Nosu with far greater confidence than would have been the case before.

'It has always seemed to me,' said Dr. Broomhall, 'that God was not going to give me that help unless I showed Him my willingness to obey in other things, and that He chose to show us His power before the adventure of faith and the experiences in Nosuland began. At Lanchow we found that caring for leprosy patients formed a large part of our work. This was a disease of which we saw little at Langchung, Szechwan, where I had worked before furlough. When we reached Nosuland and found leprosy tragically prevalent, we knew why the Lord had taken us to Lanchow first.'

Divine love is not concerned with the welfare of foreign missionaries alone! Every life is precious in His sight.

Mary Gurtler tells how God-ordered timing saved the life of a patient in the OMF Hospital at Saiburi, South Thailand.

'On arrival in Kuala Lumpur, en route to Thailand, my doctor husband, Albert, was advised that he had the wrong Thai re-entry visa. The OMF secretary there arranged to obtain the right one, and sent it to Tapah to await Albert's arrival, when he returned from settling our children in school at "Chefoo", in the Cameron Highlands.

'When he reached Tapah, the visa had not arrived, as the taxi driver bringing passengers and visa had lost his way. So he had to travel on to Butterworth without it. When the visa eventually arrived, it was too late to catch the evening train.

'Albert then planned to travel by long-distance taxi[1] across the Thai border to Yala, and get the midday train to Bangkok, but he met with delays all along the line, one reluctant taxi driver after another taking him only on stages of the journey. Another, unwilling to take only one passenger, spent over an hour drumming up other passengers in one town.

'When at last the grossly overloaded taxi left, it had travelled only forty-five minutes along the road, when a lorry, heavily laden with stones and approaching from the opposite direction, crashed into the front wing. No one was injured, but there was a long delay while the police inquired into the accident. Eventually he reached Yala, but once again too late to catch the train.

'He was greeted with the news that two new workers needed an escort to Saiburi. Would he be able to accompany them, and visit the hospital at the same time? He was delighted to have the opportunity.

'On reaching Saiburi, Albert felt compelled to go at once to the operating theatre instead of going, as in the normal course of events, straight to the doctor's house. As he walked into the theatre, the Malay patient on the

[1] At that time, as economical a method as travelling by train.

table had just stopped breathing and Dr. Clarence Yand could not get the resuscitation tube down.

'The Lord had brought Albert, a trained anaesthetist, to Saiburi at the exact moment he was needed to save the patient's life. And He had allowed the delays over visa, taxis and even a car crash for this purpose.

'Small wonder that Albert wrote in his letter to me, "What a confirmation of my call to return here, and assurance of His controlling hand even in the most frustrating circumstances".'

> *Ill that He blesses is our good,*
> *And unblest good is ill,*
> *And all is right that seems most wrong*
> *If it be His sweet will.*

The timing of the arrival of a letter had a profound effect on the evangelisation of a neglected portion of Japan.

While many missionaries of the CIM were still in China under Communist rule, seven directors of the Mission were gathered in conference at Kalorama near Melbourne, Australia. They were Bishop F. Houghton, General Director; Mr. J. R. Sinton, Deputy China Director; Rev. H. M. Griffin, Director for North America; Mr. Fred Mitchell, Director for Great Britain; Mr. J. H. Robinson, Director for South Africa; Mr. J. Oswald Sanders, Director for Australia; and Rev. H. W. Funnell, Director for New Zealand.

By this time, February 1951, the withdrawal of all missionaries from China was proceeding apace, and the question of their re-deployment was growing daily more urgent. Had the Mission now discharged its original commission to China? Should it disband? Or did the Lord of the harvest have a fresh commission for the weary band emerging from China, after years of pressure and tension? These were the perplexing questions exercising the minds of the directors.

Two days were spent in seeking God's face for guidance before formal discussions were commenced. By the end of the third day there was general agreement that it was not to be the dismal function of the Conference to recommend the disbanding of the Mission. Since its *raison d'etre* had been to work among the Chinese people, it was not a difficult decision that workers should be re-deployed in the countries of East Asia in which there were significant concentrations of overseas Chinese. It was estimated that there were at least 20,000,000 Chinese scattered among these nations.

There was one Asian country, however, about which there was considerable doubt in the minds of those gathered. Some of the directors who had been detained in China felt strongly that it would be inadvisable for the Mission to commence work in Japan at that time.

It will be remembered that General Douglas MacArthur, whose military command included Japan, had made a stirring plea for missionaries to enter that open door. Did God's plan for the CIM extend as far as Japan?

On the day when the matter was to be decided, none of the directors had any clear conviction. There was quite as much reason to expect that the decision would be against entering Japan as for it. But God had heard their earnest prayer for direction.

The morning coffee-break came while the subject of entering Japan was being discussed. With the coffee, two letters were handed to Bishop Houghton, both of which related to Japan. The writer will never forget the sense of awe that came upon those present as the General Director shared their contents with them.

The first was from a long-standing friend and supporter of the Mission, and contained a cheque for £500. He suggested that half of this sum should be used to defray the expenses of the Conference, and the remainder towards the cost of a missionary survey of Japan, if God should guide the Mission to enter that land.

The second letter came from the General Director of another missionary society whose work was in Africa. He had himself recently made a survey of the spiritual needs of Japan, and was deeply burdened for its peoples. He had endeavoured to induce his own Mission to undertake work there, but the leaders had not felt it to be God's will to embark on this new project when their hands were so fully occupied with their own large work.

He had been given the sum of US$1,400 towards the opening of the work in Japan. In his letter he said that ever since his own Mission had decided against entering Japan, they had been praying that God would lead the CIM to undertake the task. Should the directors decide that God was indeed leading them to do this, the US$1,400 would be handed over to them.

That these two letters from men of God, both of whom were concerned for the evangelisation of Japan, should arrive at the very hour when Japan was the subject of discussion, provided tangible· guidance that left little doubt in the minds of the directors as to God's will on the subject.

So Japan was included in the new outreach of the Mission. Subsequent developments in that land have abundantly demonstrated that God's guidance had not been mistaken. But for the perfect timing of the receipt of those two letters, the OMF's entry into Japan might well have been long delayed, or might never have taken place—not so much for lack of means, as for lack of assurance of God's will. God's two faithful stewards rendered a double service to the evangelisation of Japan, by sending their gifts *at exactly the right time.*

Sometimes the provision for Mission needs has arrived in a manner almost awe-inspiring, coming as it has out of the past.

In the 1940's, the annual income from some farmlands in Kansas, USA, was donated to a certain missionary society, to be used only for as long as that society was working in China. Should it cease to operate there, however, the farmlands were to become the property of the CIM.

By 1962 it had become clear that there was no prospect of that society returning to China. The property was therefore sold. The unexpended income that had accumulated from the land amounted to $23,000 and the sale realised another $40,000. An all-wise Father had reserved this magnificent sum for a time when the Mission was in great financial need. But for this provision, the missionaries would have received only one quarter of the sum that had thus become available for distribution.

'Before They Call'

DOES prayer actually influence God to change His mind? Will God reverse His purpose at our request? These are questions which challenge the praying heart.

Is not the answer that God anticipates our prayers, rather than that He changes His mind? He encourages us to bring our petitions to Him. He knows we will pray, and as someone has put it, He builds our prayers into the very structure of the universe. He has ordained that the universe should operate on a principle of personal relationships, in which He answers the prayers of His trustful children. Our heavenly Father knows what we need before we ask Him.

In the long history of the Mission there have been many incidents that demonstrate the foreknowledge of a God who is never taken by surprise. The epic story of God's provision for the interned CIM missionaries and children during the Japan-China war is one such. It is recounted in *Proving God*, but it will be to God's glory to re-tell some of the highlights for those to whom it will be new.

Had this long drawn-out period of emergency, when missionaries and children were interned for years, been foreseen, survival would have seemed utterly impossible. But God knew what lay ahead and made His preparations in good time.

It so happened that the crisis found the Mission with plenty of Chinese currency in hand—too much in fact!

The money which would normally have been expended within a few months was now tied up for the duration of the war, and Chinese currency was already in the momentum of rapid inflation. The enterprising men in the Mission's Financial Department prayed for guidance and looked for a solution to the looming crisis.

It was not long before they discovered that while they were almost embarrassed by their large stock of Chinese money, there were other missionaries and Christian organisations who were even more embarrassed by their lack of it! Sterling and US dollars they had in plenty, but it was Chinese dollars they needed to buy their daily bread and pay their outstanding accounts.

All official exchanges were closed by this time, and for many of God's servants in those days, the CIM proved to be the one place where they could obtain Chinese money. And those transactions proved to be of mutual benefit. The big sums of rapidly deteriorating Chinese money which the CIM held were being converted into currencies that would retain their value.

Now the question came of what to do with the cash that had been obtained. American and British currencies, however they might retain their value on the international exchange, were not easily negotiable in Japanese-occupied Shanghai. Japanese or Chinese paper money was subject to daily depreciation. There was only one form of currency that was always negotiable and whose value did not change—GOLD—if it could be obtained.

In the months before the missionaries were interned, the men in the financial department started buying gold. Often at considerable personal risk they made quiet forays to places where gold could be bought from Chinese merchants. They literally hazarded their lives to make provision for the needs of their fellow-workers.

Time and time again they returned to the large Sinza Road Mission Headquarters with small packets which were slipped into a hiding place behind an innocent-looking bookcase. Gold does not require much space!

Just at this juncture a group of German fellow-missionaries came to Shanghai. They were, of course, in a different category from the Americans and British. No internment camp for them! They were courteously invited by the Japanese to take up residence in a smaller compound in another part of Shanghai. As members of one of the Axis powers they were treated with respect.

Obligingly they departed to the new home allotted to them, taking their belongings with them, a large sum of money in sterling and US dollars *and the gold bars*! For the next two or three years the task that took priority over all others for some of them, was that of scouring Shanghai for inexpensive but nourishing food which they sent through the Red Cross to the missionaries and children in internment.

What this life-line meant to the internees is told by one of them:

'I think it would be true to say that but for the extra nourishment we received through the parcels sent in, some of us would not have survived the ordeal. We owe our lives to the overruling providence of God in sending that small group of German missionaries to Shanghai just before Pearl Harbour, and in enabling them to minister to us in our time of need.'

All is of God that is, and is to be;
And God is good! Let this suffice us still;
Resting in child-like trust upon His will,
Who moves to His great ends
Unthwarted by the ill.

Hardly less remarkable was the manner in which the needs of captive missionaries were supplied in advance.

On December 7th, 1941 the Japanese made their devastatingly sudden and unexpected attack on the American Base at Pearl Harbour, and Japan was at war with the USA and Britain. Some 250 CIM missionaries and 200 children were in the part of China that was occupied by the Japanese, and from that day they were virtually captives. Their sources of supply were completely cut off, and they were literally 'shut up to God'.

Despite the horrors and devastation of the blitz on London and other parts of Britain and the consequent crippling war taxation, donations to the Mission, instead of falling off, actually *increased by more than 50 per cent* over the previous year. In the USA, too, there was an increase in income of 20 per cent. This sudden increase was the Heavenly Father's quiet, unostentatious provision against the lean years that He knew lay ahead. Throughout the whole of 1941, missionaries received more than a normal allowance from this additional income.

This meant that they entered on the long years of emergency in Free China, and later captivity in the Japanese-occupied zone, with durable clothing and well-stocked larders. Although the clothing became threadbare and patched, and the cupboard often looked as bare as that of the proverbial Mother Hubbard, that early bounteous provision in a wonderful way helped to 'break the fall'.

How gracious was this timely reassurance from the One who promised, 'I will never fail you nor forsake you'.[1]

*   *   *

[1] Hebrews 13.5.

Fifty years before the emergency arose in Asia, God was moving in the heart of one of His obedient servants in the USA to provide for a need of which only He knew.

William Borden, whose life-story is told in Mrs. Howard Taylor's *Borden of Yale*,[2] was a wealthy and distinguished graduate of Yale and Princeton universities. In April 1913, he died suddenly in Cairo, where he was studying Arabic with a view to working with the CIM among the Moslems of China.

In his will, he left the greater part of his US$1,000,000 fortune to Christian missions. To the China Inland Mission, USA Branch, he bequeathed $250,000 with the suggestion that of this sum $100,000 should be invested and the income used for the care of retired missionaries in need of aid. The remainder was available for the general work of the Mission. Without this generous legacy during those war years when income was low and the rate of exchange unfavourable, the Mission would have been in serious financial straits.

Decades passed. In addition to the annual income, $45,000 of the capital of the legacy had been spent on behalf of retired missionaries and $55,000 still remained invested.

In 1958 the Mission leaders in Singapore were praying earnestly for the funds necessary to commence some of the projects in East Asia that were clamouring for attention. A large capital expenditure was involved. A mission home in Kuala Lumpur. The building of a hospital in South Thailand. A mission home in Manila. Extensions to the Language School in Singapore.

As they pondered the estimates for buildings badly needed, but for which there was no money available,

[2] Now out of print.

they little realised that a considerable portion of the required sum had been quietly coming towards them down the years.

A fresh examination had been made of the trust moneys that were being held in Philadelphia. On perusing the terms of William Borden's legacy, it was discovered that while in his will he suggested that the money be invested and the income used for retired workers, he had added another clause. This gave the Mission complete liberty to use the entire sum in any way they elected and whenever they chose.

By this time other provision had been made for retired workers, so the remaining $55,000 was quickly released for use in capital expenditures on the field. Thus the builders' hammers and the carpenters' saws were soon set to work on several of these urgent projects.

With awe and worship we realised that before 1910 when William Borden made his will, the God to whom the future is as the past knew what would be needed in 1958 and began to make provision. 'Before they call I will answer.'[3]

A reassuring experience of the pre-vision of God came to my wife and myself when we were located in Singapore.

One day the mail brought a letter addressed to my wife with the New Zealand postmark. Enclosed in the letter from a friend was a cheque for £100. 'This is for your return air fare to New Zealand', the letter ran.

This was thoroughly mystifying, for we had no intention of making a return trip to New Zealand. Our tickets had been purchased for a journey on Mission business, first to Australia for special meetings, then on to New Zealand, and thence to Canada. But it transpired that

[3] Isaiah 65.24.

this prayerful friend had not been misguided in his designation of the gift.

We travelled to Australia and were participating in a conference in a Sydney church when an urgent telephone message came through from Auckland. 'Your wife's parents are both seriously ill. Can she come immediately?' As she was the only living child, she made immediate arrangements to go. And in her purse was the cheque for £100. 'Your return air fare to New Zealand!'

Ruth Young shares a precious experience of God's provision, years in advance, for a need she could not possibly have foreseen.

'In 1960 my aunt left me a legacy,' she wrote, 'which I invested for five years, thinking I might use it for a furlough trip to visit my brother in Jerusalem. However, at the end of five years, without consulting me, the company re-invested the money for a further five years. At the end of that time I wrote asking them to withdraw the money which by then had increased to more than $2,000, and send it to me. The company urged me to re-invest, but I felt compelled to withdraw it.

'When the cheque came through for signing, I was working at the OMF Chefoo School at Nanae in Japan. Because of business I was delayed. Then a telephone call came from my sister to say that our mother was in hospital after a stroke, and could not leave the home unless someone else could help with the nursing.

'As I sat wondering what to do, the Lord said, "You have the money, there is the cheque". I immediately took a plane home.

'Owing to nursing duties, my sister had not been earning for some time, so from November 1971 to August 1972 my money and my mother's small pension met our needs. Then Mother died, and on the day of the funeral I discovered that my legacy was finished. Just enough!'

The last party of missionaries to enter China before the land was closed to missionaries in 1949, numbered forty-nine. Understandably they became popularly known as 'The Forty-niners'. Among them was a party of young people from Australia and New Zealand. Up to the date of sailing only half of the passage money required for them had been contributed. Just in time a legacy was received that more than met the need.

This was very gratifying, but the wonder of that answered prayer was revealed when it was found that *the will under which the legacy was bequeathed was made before any of the young missionaries had been born.*

The group of forty-nine flew into China on the very last external flight to carry missionaries into China. For two years they were detained in Chungking in West China under Communist rule. Their time was spent mainly in language study as there was little liberty of movement in those days.

There was one alleviating touch that revealed the tender care of a heavenly Father. Just before the party was to sail from Melbourne, a friend of the Mission in Queensland wrote to the Home Director to say that he had some warm wadded quilts that he wished to send out with the missionaries. But he had left it too late. The boat had already sailed for Brisbane.

The Home Director, however, advised him to endeavour to get them aboard the ship when it reached Brisbane. It was a close call, but they were safely shipped. The quilts entered China on the same plane as the missionaries. Was it by Divine design that when they opened the bales, to their amazement they discovered that there were—exactly forty-nine quilts. And the donor had not the faintest idea of the number of new workers.

The weather was extremely cold in Chungking that winter and, owing to war conditions, bedding was in unusually short supply. One of the forty-nine confided that but for the padded quilts they would have been a very cold group of people.

In the long history of the Mission, very large gifts have been received but rarely, and then usually in the form of legacies. But without these occasional 'heavenly windfalls' which God times for occasions of special need, we would often have been in a great crisis. When it is realised that at the time of writing more than US$200,000 are needed every month to finance its operations, the need of some larger gifts will be evident.

In 1969 we were passing through one of the periodic times of financial stringency and testing which a wise Father is pleased to permit for the strengthening of faith. Special prayer was being made in Mission centres around the world, and confidence was growing that God would intervene and meet the seemingly impossible sum required.

One morning in Philadelphia, Wayne Courtney, the Mission Treasurer in the USA, came into the author's office with a letter in his hand and made the understatement of the year. 'This is rather interesting,' he said as he handed it over.

Interesting indeed! Attached to the letter was a bank cheque for US$200,000. There was no indication of the source of the gift, nor is it known to this day. The generous anonymous donor made the stipulation that no attempt should be made to trace its source. Realising, too, that if so large a gift was made public it might tend to discourage other giving, the further stipulation was made that the gift should not be publicised. Half was designated to the medical work, and half to the evangelistic work of the OMF .

The infusion of the latter US$100,000 into the General Funds of the Mission treasury was almost enough to support the whole mission for a month. It enabled other commitments to be met, and the missionaries to receive their full allowances.

Ten years before the need for a second hostel for missionaries' children arose in Britain, a friend of the Mission donated a cottage on the condition that a retired Christian couple be allowed to occupy it during their lifetime. Mission officers kept in touch with them from time to time, but they were unaware that the wife died in January 1972 and her husband in May.

In the intervening twelve years the property had trebled in value and when sold it realised £9,000, exactly at the same time as the money was needed for the new hostel—another example of provision when the Lord, not we, knew of the need.

Enough, this covers all my need,
And so I rest,
For what I cannot, He can see
And in His care I safe shall be
For ever blessed.

Heirs of the Hundredfold

ONE of the most costly elements in missionary work, costly for both parents and children, is the frequent necessity of separation of child from parent. It is the policy of the OMF to provide primary schools on the 'field' for children of that age, where they can receive an education that will prepare them for higher education in their home country.

In the homelands the Mission provides hostels, usually staffed by missionaries, where the children can take their secondary education under conditions as much like home as possible. Some parents elect to keep their children on the field, but the majority return to the homelands.

There is no ideal solution to the problems of the care of what have come to be known as MKs—'missionary kids'! From the very nature of their parents' vocation, many of them are called upon to make sacrifices. The enforced separation can be poignant for both parents and children. In many cases, however, the parents suffer more than the children.

That our Lord envisaged the necessity for such separations for some of His followers, emerges from His words: 'Truly, I say to you, *there is no one who has left* house or brothers or sisters or mother or father or *children* or lands, for my sake and for the gospel, who will not receive an hundredfold now in this time, houses and brothers and sisters and mothers and children and lands, with persecutions, and in the age to come eternal life.'[1] For the sacrifice involved, a commensurate reward is promised.

Through the years, the CIM and later the OMF have accorded a very high priority to the care of children of its members. The schools on the field are of a high standard and are staffed by well qualified missionary teachers. But the missionaries are not alone in their concern for the children. Their Heavenly Father has demonstrated in a host of ways His own deep interest and concern, as these stories will confirm.

When Home Director in Australia, it fell to my lot to secure a suitable property as a home in Melbourne for the children of missionaries. It was a venture of faith indeed, for when the search began there was not even any money for the purpose! Faith was encouraged, however, when a legacy of £7,500 was received. But even then it was not certain that this was God's answer, for the needs of workers in the front lines must come first. £5,000 was therefore sent to Singapore for field needs. After meeting other commitments, £1,500 was left towards the hostel, and that was all.

It proved to be one of those rare occasions when there was more than sufficient to meet all field needs, so the Singapore office returned the £5,000 with instructions that it be used for the purchase of the hostel.

The £6,500 now in hand was a considerable sum in 1950, but quite insufficient at current market prices to buy a home of the required size. It must be large enough to accommodate a family of up to twenty members. The price of properties of that size ranged from £10,000 to £15,000, and nothing suitable below that figure was discovered.

When a most suitable house in the very area desired suddenly came on the market, I decided to attend the

[1] Mark 10.29, 30.

auction sale with a view to testing market values, but with no expectation of obtaining it. I had just left the Mission office in the city for the auction, when the suggestion came to mind to take a blank cheque with me, just in case the property sold for £6,500.

Bidding opened at £5,000. Then £5,500. It jumped to £6,000. Then to £6,250. With a breathed, 'Now, Lord!' I bid £6,500, the limit to which I could go. And there the bidding stopped.

The auctioneer used every artifice known to his business to coax another bid from prospective buyers, but to no avail. He was non-plussed, for such properties were bringing £10,000 and more. Saying that he could not let the property go for that ridiculous price without the consent of the owner, he withdrew for consultation.

He returned after some time and indicated that the owner was very disappointed as he had expected about twice the sum offered. However, as he had committed himself to the purchase of another property, he must sell this one. But not another bid could the auctioneer extract. The hammer came down. 'Gone for £6,500.'

The blank cheque picked up so casually at the last minute was filled in and the children at last had a very comfortable home away from home.

It is an ideal arrangement for parents at home on furlough if they can obtain accommodation near the children's hostel, so that they can see the most of their children without removing them from their school and familiar surroundings. The way in which such a home came to the Mission is an interesting story.

Prayer had been made that a property might become available in connection with the OMF hostel at Pleasant Hill, Oregon. One day Dick Cook, the house father, noticed that the house next door was up for sale, and a

most suitable home it was. But there were no funds in
hand to buy it.

He did not know, however, that just about the same
time a house in the Eastern States that had been left to
OMF was being sold, since the Mission had no use for a
house in that locality. The settlement price for the home
in Oregon amounted to $25,031.48. The settlement for
the house in Baltimore realised $25,405.58! How
parents and children rejoiced in God's heavenly
arithmetic.

The beginning of the romance of Warlingham took
place in 1948. The China Inland Mission was still in
China. In Brentwood, Essex, in England, an interested
lady friend of the Mission was considering making her
will. She owned a large Victorian house, very cold, but
with large, attractive grounds. She owned in addition
two mission halls, and wished to give the whole lot to
the Mission as a home for missionaries' children. In fact
she wanted to hand it over immediately, because there
was a possibility that the local Council might requisition
the property. The Secretary of the Mission, Rev. N. C.
Pateman, however, persuaded her that it would be best
for her to remain in her home, carry on the mission
halls, and make her will adequately in due course.

The point of interest is that God had laid this pro-
jected gift on her heart some years before it had been
decided to open a home for the children of missionaries.
The first such hostel, Maxwell House, was a rented
property in Chislehurst, Kent, opened in 1952.

The lady lived on in the house. Even when she offered
it to the Mission it was obvious that it would not suit
our purposes. During the succeeding years, while the
house deteriorated, the land increased tremendously in
value. When it was sold in 1968, the price realised was

sufficient to pay for not one but two fine hostels in which our children are now accommodated. The loving-kindness of God was making this provision twenty years before it was needed.

When the owners of Maxwell House decided to sell their property it was necessary to find new premises, and this began a long, arduous and often frustrating search. God does not always make it easy for those who are in the school of faith, but places them in positions where they must learn their lessons thoroughly.

The house desired had to be large enough to accommodate twenty children, plus a staff comprising house parents, a cook and a full time helper. The accommodation needed to be flexible enough to suit boys and girls from about ten to eighteen years of age, without recourse to dormitories.

Also desired was adequate playing space, proximity to a suitable evangelical church, adequate transport and nearness to a shopping centre. It need hardly be said that to meet these specifications it would have to be no ordinary home.

The search began in June 1967, and the house eventually chosen was purchased in July 1968. In the intervening year, hundreds of property specificaticns were studied and many homes visited all over London, with a consistent outcome. All were either too remote, too expensive, too large, or otherwise unsuitable.

On December 29th, 1967, Mr. Pateman inspected a promising property at Warlingham, Surrey, called 'Bromfield'. It was a beautifully warm and lovely home. He came away with two vivid impressions. One was that it was easily the best property he had inspected. The other was created by the caretaker's parting words : 'I hear that the owner, who is a millionaire, wants

£75,000 for the lot.' £75,000! Completely beyond anything he could envisage!

'But,' he thought, 'if the property could be sub-divided, and we did not have to take the whole, would the owner be willing to sell? A telephone call brought the startling news that he would sell the part we desired for £27,500—not so daunting a figure as £75,000.

Members of the OMF Council inspected the property, but there was a considerable divergence of opinion. There were three main causes for the reservations of some. First, the bedrooms were not ideally suited to our purposes. Second, the subdivision left the grounds too small. Third, the place seemed too luxurious for missionaries' children. 'It would be all right for a film star', said one Council member.

Meanwhile, other properties were inspected, and other people were looking at 'Bromfield'. Among those who nearly bought it was the Madame Curie Foundation.

Months passed by, and Maxwell House would have to be vacated by September at the latest. Once again the Home Director and the Secretary viewed 'Bromfield', and returned with the conviction that this was indeed God's choice for the hostel. It was eventually decided to buy, and an offer of £24,000 was made. One of the objections had been removed, as the owner had agreed to include extra land.

But the offer came too late. As the property had been on the market for a year without a sale, the owner had decided to auction it. When at long last the OMF's offer was made, he said, 'Well, I've gone so far with the auction that is due to come up in a few days' time, I would rather not sell it now'.

The auction was held and the property was knocked down to the OMF, not for £24,000 but for £20,000! Was it not amazing that a property so desirable as this one, in a select area just on the edge of London should remain vacant for about a year, and that the Mission should be able to secure it at such a ridiculously low figure? Surely, it was the Lord who had reserved it for the purpose of His work. 'Who can utter the mighty doings of the Lord, or show forth all His praise?'[2]

Does the property meet the desired specifications? Indeed it does. Downstairs there are living rooms ample for all occasions, and a large modern kitchen. There is oil-fired central heating, a cold store, a deep freeze, six baths and nine toilets. There are two large lawns and playing space. It is close to a good evangelical church. Two railway stations are within three-quarters of a mile, and it is close to shopping. It is sited on the brow of a hill and has magnificent views, and delightful walks almost from the very door.

As to furniture and fittings, the house was carpeted throughout, there were curtains on all the windows and in some rooms there were chandeliers too elaborate for a children's hostel. All these were sold to the OMF for £1,000, much of which was regained by the sale of the chandeliers. So God gave a magnificent home in answer to the trembling prayers of His children.

Although the property was known as 'Bromfield', it was renamed 'Maxwell House', since that stood not just for a building left behind, but a community carried forward in which 'Old Maxwellians' still shared with new arrivals.

In retrospect it will be seen that God had something much wider and bigger in view than just finding a house. It must be a house that would be a testimony to Him today. Not just to the God of Hudson Taylor but to the living God who is 'the same today', who does wonders for those who trust Him.

[2] Psalm 106.2.

It proved to be an experience that will never be forgotten by the young people concerned. They saw God doing wonders in their own day.

The small OMF school in the Philippines caters for both English-speaking and German-speaking children. When the school was moved from Calapan to Baguio in 1970, a house large enough to accommodate the English-speaking section was rented. But more bedrooms and a class room were needed for the German-speaking children.

The second house would be used for the three class-rooms and the teachers' quarters. It would need to be situated near by, so that teachers and pupils could come and go easily, especially in the rainy weather of which Baguio has much more than its share during the summer months.

A thorough search produced no results. The house-father instituted inquiries about the house next door, which was a student boarding-house. But he was told it was not available for sale or lease.

One day the owner of that house was in Manila and a further approach was made. This time it was discovered that he was most interested in renting it to OMF! Permission was readily given to put a gate through into the other school building.

Now the school had exactly the accommodation required according to the plan. As a bonus, the area beside the school had been cemented just a couple of months previously and made a fine playing area that does not get muddy in the rainy season.

The care and concern of God for these children who are deprived to some extent of the physical expression of their parents' affection, extends far beyond the provision of comfortable homes. The Lord's words through Isaiah, 'As one whom his mother comforts, so I will comfort you',[3] clearly intimate that there are in Him the attributes of motherhood as well as of fatherhood. He both knows the pangs of a mother-heart for her suffering child, and is not indifferent to the child's distress. One missionary mother shares her experience of His sympathetic provision :

'God had blessed us with a little daughter, Judith, who was born with a defect in her mouth which would require surgery in several stages', writes Daphne Gibson. 'We little realised what precious lessons of His wonderful and timely financial supply we were to learn through this unwelcome necessity.

'The first operation took place when she was eight months old. Not being conversant with hospital costs and doctors' fees in the Philippines, we thought we might scrape through on our meagre bank balance. The mission remittance for that quarter was very low.

'I went to the hospital with Judy, as a "watcher", and as I had to stay for eight days without relief, we took a private room. Three days after the operation, I enquired the amount of our account to date. To my dismay I discovered that the hospital bill had already exceeded our available money and there were still five more days in hospital, plus the doctor's fee.

'We were allowed to leave the hospital without paying the hospital bill which was sent to the OMF office. By the time we reached there, we had received unexpected personal gifts from South Africa and England which not only met the whole bill, but left us with some money for Christmas, which was just around the corner.

'The wonderful thing was that most of the money had been given before we even knew that Judy would be

[3] Isaiah 66.13.

having the operation at that time, and it came from people who did not know that there was anything wrong with her. It was a clear case of, "before they call, I will answer".

'The cost of the second operation five months later, was met by similar special provision. The third operation which took place two years later proved to be twice as expensive. Again we asked the inevitable, "How?" and again the Lord provided in a wonderful way.

'One of our fellow-missionaries had received a considerable legacy. As she was asking the Lord what she should do with it, He touched her heart to pay for the whole operation.

'We are still seeing the Lord supplying Judy's medical needs. She has now developed a cross-bite and is under the orthodontist for long drawn out and expensive treatment. The special brace alone cost 200 *pesos*. Just before we had to pay for it, we received out of the blue a gift more than sufficient, from a man whom we had met only once.

'It is such a joy to share with our little daughter, who is now eight years old, just how much the Lord has cared for her. She is old enough now to appreciate this.'

The same loving Father is not indifferent to the prayers of little children, and is interested in teaching them the reality of prayer.

Brian and Daphne were feeling the need of a jeep so that they could be more mobile in their work, and thus reach more people for the Lord. As they prayed for this, gifts began to flow in.

'We told our three-year-old son that we were praying for a jeep, and encouraged him to join us. How he prayed, and how he believed that God would answer his prayers! I'm sure it was through his simple faith that three months later we had sufficient to pay for the jeep.

'A few days before we actually purchased it, Gavin asked me, "Mummy, where is heaven?" I tried to explain that it is where God is, somewhere called "beyond the sky". That night he prayed, "Dear God, when you send our jeep, please don't drop it out of heaven. It might break. Would you please just put it in our back garden."

'A few mornings later, when he woke up, there was the jeep in the back garden!'

Not all God's provision for the children of missionaries comes in a spectacular way, yet it is no less *His* provision. Norman Pateman, whose special sphere of concern this has been, explains how God has used the Education Authorities in Britain to make generous provision for the education and welfare of British children.

After the age of eleven the children normally return to Britain. Because of special grants made by the Government, these children and others similarly placed are able to attend boarding schools. Without these grants, support costs would be much higher than many parents could afford.

Two or three years ago the grants, which vary from area to area, came through an Authority which perhaps did not keep pace with rapidly rising fees and prices. The disparity between grant and bill for fees became alarmingly wider.

Around the time when this position was causing increasing concern, it was necessary for the hostel to be moved to different premises which became available at that time. The new hostel is located in an area supervised by a different Local Education Authority. Not only did this Authority assume responsibility for the boys and girls returning home to the hostel, but without any request from the Mission, they took over payment of grants made by the former Authority. And what is more, these grants were on a far more generous scale than had previously been the case.

The truth of the promise, 'Before they call, I will answer', has been illustrated in a previous chapter. But this particular incident carries it a stage further, *'without their calling, I will answer'*.

The Romance of Property

THE miracles of our Heavenly Father's provision of 'houses and lands' have been by no means limited to meeting the needs of the children of the Mission. Offices and homes of many kinds have also been supplied.

It did not seem very romantic at the time. Hours and days spent tramping around dusty streets in tropical heat, seeking in vain for suitable premises in which to carry on the work of God was a very prosaic assignment for those engaged in it! The men who trudged the streets of Singapore in 1952 certainly did not find their task romantic—until God intervened in such a dramatic way that weariness and frustration were soon banished.

Following the Mission's withdrawal from China, the new headquarters of the China Inland Mission Overseas Missionary Fellowship had been set up in a twenty-roomed boarding house in Chancery Lane, Singapore. By this time the stream of returning missionaries was beginning to flow strongly and before long, as with Elisha's school of the prophets, the place was too small to accommodate them. So a search was instituted for more commodious and suitable premises.

The need for a permanent Language School for those who were facing the challenge of entirely new languages and conditions added urgency to the search. If new premises could be found, the Chancery Lane building lent itself admirably to the purposes of a Language School.

Eventually an eminently suitable site was located, but

the asking price was far beyond anything the Mission could afford. The property was situated opposite Singapore's famed Botanical Gardens—two acres of developed land with a seven-bedroomed house and plenty of land on which to erect offices and flats. The airy living rooms of the house were ideal for a mission home.

Gifts were coming in, designated for new buildings in Singapore. But when tentative enquiries were made, it was discovered that the sale price of the property was 170,000 Malay dollars, more than twice as much as was in hand for the new headquarters. The desirable plot seemed unattainable, and yet, was this beyond God's power to supply? Prayer was constantly being made about the matter, and God was working.

One day the real-estate agent telephoned saying that he thought the owners of the property might sell for M$105,000—a sudden drop of M$65,000! It was a most tempting offer, for the property was well worth the price originally asked. Had there been M$105,000 in the Building Fund, the offer would without doubt have been readily accepted. But there was only M$85,000 available.

'We can give M$85,000 for the property and no more', said Rowland Butler, the Mission representative.

'I only have power of attorney to accept M$90,000', replied the agent.

It was no use. There just was not that extra M$5,000 in hand. The telephone receiver was replaced rather sadly. To be so near obtaining so eminently suitable a property, so urgently needed, and then to lose it just for lack of M$5,000!

But the transaction was still in God's hands, and the lack of M$5,000 was no problem to Him. He just brought the price down! The telephone bell rang less than five minutes after the receiver had been replaced.

'Take the thing!' said a rather irate voice at the other end of the wire. 'Take it for M$85,000!'

And so the money that had been coming in, much of it contributed by members of the Mission whose own purses were by no means overfull, proved sufficient after all.

It is worthy of note that the adjoining undeveloped block of land had just been purchased for M$2 per square foot while the Mission property was obtained for exactly half that price, with the large house thrown in!

There was another gracious evidence of a Father's overruling in this transaction. When the offices and apartment buildings were being erected on the newly purchased Cluny Road property, the block of land two doors away was also being prepared for the erection of apartments. Work began on both properties about the same time, but the neighbour's property was found to require extensive and costly pile driving. It took them a whole year to lay the foundations alone. No piling was necessary on the Mission property, and all the buildings were completed before the foundations of the other building had been laid.

And what of the property today? The offices and apartments have served the Mission well for twenty years. Meanwhile the commercial centre of Singapore has been moving out towards the Botanical Gardens, and the property has multiplied many times in value. The confidence reposed in God was not misplaced.

The story of the South African headquarters of the OMF in Cape Town was no less romantic.

To mark the centenary of the China Inland Mission in 1965 special prayer objectives were adopted in different parts of the world. The Council of the South African branch, youngest of the home centres at that time, was impressed to pray for a much-needed mission home as a base for the growing work. As more South Africans joined the ranks of the Mission the need became increasingly urgent, but no funds were available for this purpose.

Quite unexpectedly the spacious, though old, Andrew Murray Missionary Home was offered by the Trustees to any mission that would undertake to maintain it for the use of missionaries and as a place of prayer. With gratitude to God and to the Trustees, the Council gratefully accepted the property on the stated terms.

Situated as it was on a magnificent site overlooking the beautiful Cape Town harbour, despite its drawbacks the old home was known and loved by many. In course of time the increasing deterioration of the buildings and the changing needs of a growing Mission necessitated a more modern home, as well as additional accommodation for furlough and Home Staff workers. Then, too, there was need of a hostel for missionaries' children who were remaining at home for their education.

After much prayer and deliberation it was finally decided that any move should be to the southern suburbs which have easy access to schools, the main churches and the majority of interested friends. This decision was not difficult to reach, but it was another matter to locate the right site.

Over a period of six months many properties were inspected, but there was always some snag, or some aspect that was less than ideal. Despite this, Council members shared the strong conviction that God had the perfect place, although it was not revealed as yet.

'The Chairman of the OMF Council at that time was also Chairman of the YWCA', wrote Sylvia Houliston, wife of the Home Director. 'The latter body was also searching for more suitable premises for their own work. After long and fruitless search, they reached the conclusion that the Andrew Murray Home property would be the ideal site on which to erect their new youth hostel. Then suddenly the YWCA encountered a serious legal problem in the sale of their own property, and what had seemed a mutually satisfactory sale was checkmated.

'One morning we decided to pray especially for the property needs of the YWCA, and as a result felt that we should halt our search and wait until they were given the green light. Then the telephone rang with the offer of a property. Should we refuse to inspect a site that seemed so suitable?

'On reaching Claremont we saw a beautiful home on a corner site, large enough for our needs, with ample land for another flat and office accommodation. It was near to transport, schools, churches and shops. Across the road was a municipal playing field which leads into the Claremont Botanical Gardens. Our search had ended.

'We determined to secure an option to purchase, but we were too late. Another agent had secured an option for a speculator. But God kept it for us. Council members, however, could not see their way to buy it unless the YWCA purchased our old property.

'My husband was heart-broken. Had God shown us the ideal property only to let us lose it? Gradually peace returned, and another option was taken. At a remarkable Council meeting, doubts were dispelled and these godly men decided to move forward in faith. It was a step of faith indeed, for at that point we did not have available the amount required even for the down-payment.

'The YWCA Committee met the next morning. Could they, too, step forward in faith to purchase the OMF Home, when there seemed no prospect of selling their other property? God brought them to unity of mind that this was His will for them, and they too committed themselves to a step of faith. Remarkably enough they had in their building fund just sufficient for us to purchase the Claremont property, and the remainder of the purchase price was to be paid a year later.

'Our estate agent, an interested and amazed spectator said, "It was as if you threw all the pieces of a jig-saw puzzle into the air, and they all came down in the correct places!"

'The old home had realised 85,000 *Rand* and the new property had cost R51,000. We had only R35,000 that could be spent on the new flat. Tenders were called and, as prices were rising, it was with trepidation that we opened the tenders. The first three were far above our limit. Then the fourth was opened—for R34,980!

'To God alone the glory!'

The story of the unusual circumstances surrounding the provision of much needed premises in Japan is told by missionary-architect David Highwood.

'It was in 1955 when suitable and conveniently located property was extremely difficult to procure in Tokyo, except at an exorbitant price. An exhaustive search had failed to locate anything within the very limited amount of money available. God moved a Christian Japanese business man to make a small but suitable property available to the OMF at a very generous price. This small home served as the Mission's headquarters for many years.

'The district in which it is situated, however, has now become the fashionable residential area for top business executives and TV types. The value of residential property has inevitably soared. More space was needed for OMF operations, but planning permission for additional building was withheld. There was also the urgent need for a hostel for the children of missionaries who were attending a Christian secondary school. So a new search for premises began.

'About two months later, a Christian real-estate agent brought to our notice a property as good as new, and within easy reach of this school. There was a spacious garden and ample room for building the required hostel. Moreover, it had been built with all modern fittings and, as the previous owner had been a tall man, all doorways were higher than is usual in a Japanese home—a boon to the big western missionaries.

'Within a month—this was in 1972—the price which had been set for the old property had been paid over. This completely covered the cost of the new property and agents' fees, and in addition the surplus was sufficient to erect the proposed hostel and cover removal costs—with some to spare.

'The timing too, was perfect. Everything was beyond expectations. Everyone who sees the place expresses pleasure and thankfulness to God for His gracious provision. He does not always see fit to treat us like this, but when He does, we should not be surprised.'

Another joyous surprise came to Anna Douglas when she and her husband were living in Manila.

'We had been asked to assume responsibility for the Chinese Youth Gospel Centre in the heart of Manila's Chinatown. Having two little toddlers, the problem of where we should live in this crowded city was an acute one. We really needed some place with a yard and a fence.

'One day I sighted the ideal place. It was very near the church we attended, and was ideal for our purpose. I mentioned the place to my husband. His immediate reaction was, "You do not know the landlord, the present occupants or the exorbitant rent they may charge an Americano".

'My response was, "That's the very place we need, and whoever lives there, we can pray them out!" Alban was horrified. Never would he join me in such a petition as to pray someone out of their home!

'So sure was I that this was God's home for us, that I began praying alone. Day in and day out I prayed, "Lord, you know we need a home, and this place is suitable. Whoever is living there, please make them move."

'A week went by and nothing happpened. My faith began to waver. I heard the whispered suggestion, "You are rather foolish to pray like this when you know nothing about the owners, etc.". I conceded it was a bit stupid, but I continued praying, "Lord, whoever lives there, make them move".

'Two weeks went by. One day I received a message from a missionary, "If you want that place, you can have it. The folk living there have suddenly moved!"

'I was the only one who could explain that sudden move. Guess who humbled himself and moved in with me?

'That's right. He did!'

In 1972, the need arose for a hostel for the children of our Australian missionaries. It was decided to adapt the OMF Mission Home in Sydney for this purpose. This however meant that the State Secretary and his wife, Mr. and Mrs. E. W. Norgate, would be without a home. They were cast on the Lord—'a very good place to be cast', as the Home Director said.

Mr. Norgate 'happened' to meet an acquaintance in the street one day. In answer to a question, this friend said he had recently gone into the real estate business.

No, his firm did not handle properties for rent. He had, however, just heard of someone who was seeking a tenant for a house in Turramurra, the very suburb in which the Mission Home and office were situated! Ten days before their deadline, the Norgates moved into their new home.

This was not the long-term answer to the need, but it gave a respite of six months while other premises were being found. One friend provided a removal van, while others prepared the house and grounds. But finding a builder to undertake the alterations to the Home at a reasonable figure proved surprisingly difficult.

Just when the search seemed hopeless, a builder friend returned from a trip abroad, heard of the need and offered to do the job on an acceptable basis. So on the same day as the Norgates moved, the bricks began to fall and the dust to fly, and the hostel for the children began to take shape.

The property needs of a Christian Publishing House are just as much the matter of a heavenly Father's interest and concern as homes for His children. The way in which OMF Publishers were providentially led to ideally suitable premises in crowded Manila, brought great encouragement to members of the staff.

The need for a building better adapted to the needs of the wholesale department was growing more urgent. God guided His servants to a property in every way ideal for its purpose.

The building was situated on the corner of Marquez de Comillas and Oregon Streets, only one minute distant from the OMF Mission Home, three minutes away from the OMF office, and only five minutes walk from the retail book store. It was on the ground floor, flood-free (an important factor in Manila) with a back entrance for bringing in supplies. The building, of concrete with a good *terazzo* floor and concrete ceiling, was in good condition.

The manager, John de Kock, said that they themselves would never have discovered the place, for it was occupied. He had placed an advertisement in the paper, and the landlady had called to tell them about it.

The remarkable feature was that it required the three existing tenants to move out, to give OMF Publishers the building. Two of them had gone bankrupt and were waiting for a sub-tenant to take over before the landlady would let them move out. But the evacuation was safely accomplished.

Another wonderful provision was a telephone. When one realises that it often takes years to secure a telephone in Manila, the good hand of God upon His work is clearly seen.

'Even to Old Age'[1]

FOR those who have spent their lives in the service of the Lord in foreign lands, and have had no opportunity of making provision for their old age, the approach of retirement might well cause apprehension. Who is to care for them when they are no longer able to care for themselves?

The call of God has often involved the foregoing of marriage, and the experience of many retired missionaries echoes the words of F. W. H. Myers in his *St. Paul*:

> *On without cheer of sister or of daughter,*
> *Yes, without stay of father or of son,*
> *Lone on the land and homeless on the water,*
> *Pass I in patience till my work is done.*

But the God who is better than a husband and sticks closer than a brother does not fail to appreciate the sacrifice willingly made for His sake, nor does He leave them without provision for their declining days.

Had the choice of a home for the British retired missionaries been left to themselves, they would never have looked for anything as wonderful as the home God provided for them. Something far less imposing in a vastly inferior neighbourhood would have seemed adequate from their point of view.

But if God chose to make this generous gift, should

[1] Isaiah 46.4.

not they accept it with joy and gratitude? In the event, they learned to know Him as the God 'who gives us all things richly to enjoy'.

The story of Cornford House is told in *Proving God*, and will be familiar to many older friends of the Mission, but it is included here so that new readers may share its blessing.

Sixty years ago the majority of members of the Mission came from Great Britain, with the consequence that there are more retired workers there than in the other sending countries. The corollary is that there is a greater need for accommodation. By 1953 the need had become urgent. The Retired Workers' Home envisaged would need to provide accommodation for about thirty people, several of whom could walk about only with difficulty. Thus if the house was of more than one storey, a lift would be necessary.

The neighbourhood of Tunbridge Wells was considered the most desirable, but the money in hand was very limited and property in that area was highly priced. Many homes were inspected, but they were either too dilapidated, too inconvenient, too far from London or much too expensive.

Then, quite suddenly it seemed, God drew the curtain back and disclosed a house far better than had been dreamed possible! An urgent telegram addressed to the Rev. George Scott, later to become Home Director for Great Britain, read:

> 'There is a house to suit you at Pembury. Others are interested but the owner will defer a decision until you have seen it. Telephone Pembury immediately.'

He did so, and the following day travelled to Pembury,

which is two miles from the centre of Tunbridge Wells. He walked up a wide, sweeping drive to a long, three-storeyed house whose terraced lawns ran down to a beech hedge, beyond which stretched meadows, trees and hills, right to the sky-line.

The owner was a Christian lady who, since she had to dispose of her home, desired greatly that it should be used as a home for elderly people connected with some Christian organisation. She was offering it to such at a price far below market value. And the house had a lift! It all seemed too good to be true, but it *was* true.

The lady of the house had known nothing of the China Inland Mission and the need of the retired missionaries when she decided to sell her house. Indeed, she had another organisation in mind when she first offered it at that very low price, and was greatly disappointed when her offer was not accepted. She had almost despaired of seeing her home used in the way she desired and had already put it in the hands of agents, when one night she was suddenly awakened.

The thought of the house was still in her mind and, almost as clearly as if she heard a Voice, the thought came, 'Write to Tom Rees'. She did not know Mr. Rees, but she wrote to him the next day, asking if he knew of a Christian organisation requiring such a place as 'Cornford House'.

He knew of none, but got in touch with a friend in a firm of building contractors. The friend knew of none, but his secretary did! She had heard that the CIM was looking for a home for retired workers, for she had been asked a few weeks previously if she knew of such a place! And so the links in the chain were complete. The owner of Cornford House was brought in touch with the CIM, and within a month the house became the property of the Mission.

It so happened that the income of the Mission was unusually low at that time, but money had already been contributed from various sources especially for a home for retired missionaries, so the purchase of the beautiful estate was possible. Extensive alterations were necessary, however, and no money could be spared from the General Fund for these. But that was not allowed to hinder matters. It became quite evident that the Lord was making Cornford House, in a peculiar way, His responsibility.

Gifts specially designated for the home trickled in in a steady stream—on one occasion, at a time when unexpected expenses were looming up, £5,000 were received specifically for 'Cornford House'. Furniture and equipment came from all sort of unexpected sources. And when on September 3rd, 1954 Cornford House was officially opened, every expense had been met, quite apart from the General Fund of the Mission.

God's bountiful provision for His ageing servants was not confined to the United Kingdom. In the United States, too, an increasing number of retired missionaries had reached the stage of life when they were no longer able to care for themselves. They had been living in Mission-provided apartments in Philadelphia, but now the need for a home where they could be lovingly ministered to had become a pressing necessity.

In the providence of God, an evangelical church with a vital missionary interest and special concern for the elderly was just embarking on a scheme to construct a village with a hospital attached for aged Christians. The moving spirit in the project was a long-standing friend of OMF who was aware of this need of accommodation for retired missionaries. What could be more appropriate than to invite OMF to erect the home for their older workers as part of the village complex?

The village is situated in beautiful Lancaster, Pennsylvania, in an attractive semi-rural setting, yet close to the city. More important, it is within easy walking distance of the church that sponsored the project. The fact that the village scheme included a Christian hospital was an added attraction. Should they become ill, medical care would be available.

The proposal was warmly welcomed by the OMF Council, but there was a financial obstacle to be overcome, and it was no small one. True, there was a sum of money in hand for the purpose, but it was far from adequate for the large expenditure that would be involved. Recourse was made to the prayer of faith.

On the other side of the continent, a loyal friend and supporter of the Mission had lost her life-partner. Her links with the Mission were very close, through a relative who had served with the CIM in China and with whom she now lived. The news of the proposed home came to her ears. What better memorial to her husband could she have than a part in this Retired Workers' Home?

The generous impulse prompted by a warm heart and the moving of the Spirit of God found expression in a gift of $50,000. With other money donated, this was sufficient to complete the project. Many elderly missionaries who had suffered hardship in disturbed and war-torn China, have thanked God for the comfort and loving care they have enjoyed at *Lammermuir*, Lancaster, Pennsylvania.

It sometimes happens, however, that God is pleased to deliver His children, not *from* the hour of trial, but *out of it*. Glory is brought to Him when, instead of sliding out from beneath it, we bear up under it.

An up-to-date illustration of this truth demonstrates that God cannot prove false to His faithfulness, even though He may allow His servant to be severely tested. The story was written for *The Life of Faith* by a retired OMF missionary who had recently lost her husband.

'Today the rent-man was due, and sure enough the quarterly cheque from the OMF headquarters arrived by the first post, my share of the Lord's loving provision. My heart was singing in worship and adoration as I went down in the bus to the bank; in my purse there was still the "handful of meal"—seven-pence for the bus fare, two-pence for the receipt and six-pence left over.

'Two-and-a-half weeks ago my son went abroad to work for the summer, leaving me alone in the house. The phone bill was in and enough money to pay it with a few shillings over, so it seemed right to get that settled and see what the Lord would do with this "handful of meal". I was expecting a handsome gift from someone (though I did not know who the Lord would use), but it did not turn out that way. All through this time there was never more than a few shillings in the purse, but there was always something.

'Of course food is not such a problem when the family is away and first I ate up what was in the cupboard, together with a big helping of cabbage from the garden. It came to the weekend with only the cabbage left (and the daily order of milk for me and the cat), so I definitely asked the Lord for some dinner. Soon N. phoned to say she had been given a chicken and would I come and share it! Not only that, but she gave me a shopping-bag of food, so that I was able to invite a friend of my son's to tea on Sunday and have something with the cabbage each day.

'The coffee went down (one of my favourite things),

but I had been given a good supply of tea previously and it was a joy to accept what the Lord had provided, as I realised how often there had been an element of greed in my own choice.

'Meanwhile the Billy Graham Crusade was on, with the seven-penny bus fare each way into town. When needed the money was there; sometimes a neighbour asked to use the phone or buy a stamp and there was six-pence or four-pence, and often a kind neighbour gave me a lift as he was a steward in the Crusade and I was counselling. He waited for me until I was free to come home.

'On the Friday the cupboard was pretty bare again, but there was enough for a loaf, and two friends who came home to tea after the Ladies Prayer Meeting brought country eggs with them. But when two young members of the family came in from a distance, my mind flew to breakfast with only one egg left after we had all had tea; however, I went across to tell my neighbour that I would have to go down later as folk had come in, and his wife at once asked how I was off for food and gave me bacon and extra milk.

'The following morning the young man had the one egg, and the young lady said it was the best breakfast she had had all the holiday as eggs did not agree with her and bacon and tomato did! My friend N. invited me back to dinner on the second Saturday, and did not realise why I hesitated when she asked me for Sunday too—it was just the matter of the bus fare!

'One thing that I had been really grieved about, and a bit embarrassed too, was not having anything to put in the offering on Sunday, or night by night at the Crusade; I told the Lord about it, and asked Him for something extra that I might give—and on the Saturday afternoon, quite "out of the blue", I sold two copies of a book and so had money for the offering and weekend expenses.

'Of course, the cat had to be feed whatever the stringency, and when the kind butcher gave me a bag of scraps of liver for her, I eyed them as the prodigal son did the "husks that the swine did eat"! However, I was a spoilt child of the Father and not a prodigal, so the cat and I shared a delicious dinner of her fresh liver! A present of fish from one of the Scripture Union girls provided high tea for a friend of my son's who had been converted at the Crusade, and she brought farm eggs with her; and so the testing time finished.

'For years my husband and I have been members of a "Faith Mission" and have many times received special personal provision as well as that through the Mission "family", but this experience has been outstanding in that I was facing it alone, where I used to depend so much on my husband's wisdom and experience and faith. I was brought low before the Lord, but now I can say, "Where is the Lord God of Elijah, or George Müller and the other heroes of faith?" and humbly answer, "*He is the same*, yesterday, today and for ever", and still provides a handful of meal in a barrel and a little oil in a cruse for a widow-woman and her friends.'

My need was known
To Thee alone—
I called upon Thy name;
No other heard
Prayer's whispered word
And yet the answer came.

Thus secretly,
'Twixt me and Thee,
Let traffic grow apace,
That even I
May testify
To Thine exceeding grace.

F. Houghton

The Versatility of God

GOD can use even a temperamental oil well to meet the needs of His work!

Mr. and Mrs. Hubert Fisher, OMF missionaries from Japan, were guests of a gracious Christian couple in a Californian city. 'It's fine to be a Christian, living in California and owning an oil well,' Mr. Fisher laughingly said to his hostess.

' "That is all true of us," she replied, "but although the well next to ours gushes out thousands of dollars worth of oil each month, ours produces very little. In fact, the last time it produced 13 cents worth!"

'She went on to tell us, however, of a time when they needed $1,000 for their children's education. Just then the oil well gushed out exactly $1,000 worth of oil. On another occasion, they had a medical need of $500. That time the well's contribution was $500.

'Our host was a quiet man, but suddenly his eyes sparkled and he said enthusiastically, "When my oil well really gets going, I'll build you a church".

'Next morning our host's chair was empty at the breakfast table, and his wife explained that he had gone to visit his oil well in the desert. When he returned late at night, it was to tell us that the well had produced exactly —64 cents worth of oil!

'In 1968 we commenced work in Iwamizawa, a Japanese city with a population of 70,000. We began to visit houses, offices, homes, hospitals and schools in the city, distributing *Every Home Crusade* tracts. In the district allocated to us there was a new housing project known as "Sunrise". Land had been reserved for a Buddhist temple, but no place for any other religion.

'No home was available in this area which housed 20,000 people, so we began to pray for funds for a building. To our dismay, our doctor ordered us home for retirement. Our disappointment was tempered by delight that a young couple from the Philippines came to Iwamizawa to work. But they were unable to procure a home in "Sunrise" and were living in a rented house in another suburb.

'Now back to California where the oil wells are! Our host of that weekend died without seeing his oil well "come in", but his wife sent a fine gift as a memorial to him. His son also began to send in gifts. A few months ago the largest gift he had ever sent was received and, as was our habit, it was sent at once to Japan.

'In acknowledging the gift, the Superintendent wrote that as they had found it impossible to rent a home in "Sunrise", they were planning to use the money to purchase a piece of land, and to build there a church to be a lighthouse for our Lord Jesus Christ.

'Moral—truly a good son is worth more than a temperamental oil well.'

The author has good reason to be grateful to God for His intervention in extricating him from an impossible situation.

During a tour of OMF fields, I was travelling from Taiwan to Japan. I did not usually carry much currency on such journeys, as I could collect the currency of each country I was visiting from the Mission office. On this occasion, when I arrived in Tokyo I had less than US$10.

I had arranged to be met at the Tokyo airport, but on

arrival I found no one there to meet me and concluded that there had been some delay. This was about 8.45 p.m. After waiting an hour, action seemed called for, so I changed my dollars into *yen*, and telephoned the three or four people whom I knew in Tokyo. In each case the response was the same, all were away from home on holiday. All my contacts were exhausted.

Then I telephoned the OMF centre at Karuizawa, about fifty miles away. Once again the missionary was not at home. I asked the Japanese friend who answered the telephone where I could stay that night in Tokyo, as I did not know the city. He suggested Hotel Marounouchi. I spelled the name back over the telephone to ensure that I had it correct.

Tokyo is a city of about ten million people, and the taxi-fare from airport to city made alarming inroads into my little store of *yen*. It was approaching midnight when I reached the hotel—only to find that no rooms were available. I enquired whether I could spend the night in one of the chairs in the lounge, but that was not permissible.

In desperation I asked if there was not a room of any kind available. The receptionist replied, 'Well there is one room, but the central heating is defective and the room is too hot'. I immediately said I would take it, despite the heat.

On my asking the cost, the receptionist said he would reduce the price. The sum asked was exactly what I had left. I would not have been able to pay for a good room in any case !

I lay in bed praying and perspiring—in a perfect *cul-de-sac*, shut up to God.

Alone and penniless in a city of ten million. I was supposed to leave early in the morning for a conference in northern Japan. I knew no one, and no one knew where I was. Whence could deliverance come?

Suddenly the telephone at my bedside rang, and a voice said, 'Is that you, Mr. Sanders?' 'Yes, who is speaking?' 'David Hayman', came the reply. My feelings can be imagined.

There had been a misunderstanding about the time of arrival of the plane. David thought it was due to arrive at 11.45 p.m. and was there in good time. When he discovered that my plane had arrived at 8.45 p.m., he searched everywhere to find the missing passenger.

Just as he was about to abandon the search, he decided to make a last inquiry at the telephone counter. One of the attendants volunteered the information that a foreigner had telephoned Karuizawa, and he had heard him spell out Marounouchi. Perhaps it would be worthwhile inquiring at Hotel Marounouchi!

How impossible—and yet how simple a solution. I caught the early morning train and arrived at the conference in time, immeasurably enriched by an up-to-date experience of the superintending providence of God.

> *So do we stand as ancient Israel stood,*
> *The sea before us and the foe behind,*
> *Forced to advance into the whelming flood,*
> *Trusting an unseen Hand the waves to bind;*
> *Led thro' the darkness by His staff and rod,*
> *A cloud before us, and within it, God.*

It is not difficult to discern the hand of God when all is running smoothly, but it is not so easy when adversity strikes.

Two missionaries returning to England with their four small children were detained in Canada owing to war conditions. Suddenly they found themselves penniless.

The furnished house that had been so wonderfully provided for them was broken into and all their money stolen. Apart from a small supply of groceries and a few cents they had in their pockets, they had nothing—and it was several weeks before they could expect their next remittance from the Mission.

Very earnestly the young couple made their petitions to their heavenly Father that night. This was a test of faith indeed—and a test of God's faithfulness. How would He meet their needs now? They were soon to see!

The following day a box of provisions was delivered at their door. There was no indication from whom it had come, but the bill was paid and the goods addressed to them. That gift saw them through the next two or three days, and then a letter arrived for them from a friend in England—containing a cheque.

Now as it happened, financial restrictions had been imposed in England, forbidding money being sent out of the country privately. The missionaries' friend, however, knew nothing of these restrictions and sent the cheque in good faith. The missionaries knew nothing about the restrictions, either, and went joyfully to the bank to cash the cheque. The most remarkable part of this story perhaps is that not even the bank clerk knew of the new regulations and he cashed the cheque without demur.

Not until some weeks later was the mistake discovered. They were then required to refund the money. But by this time they were in a position to do so, having received their quarterly remittance. That innocent mistake had been God's provision to meet the emergency caused by the theft.

The average membership of Japanese churches is very

small, with the result that the purchase of land and the erection of a church is almost beyond the powers of these small groups. To help them in their problem, the Hokkaido Evangelical Churches Association established a Revolving Building Fund. One of the beneficiaries was the church at Kutchan which had come into being through the work of OMF missionaries.

Mrs. Nakata had been a member of the Kutchan church for a number of years when she moved away from the area with her husband. She maintained her membership, however, and from time to time sent considerable contributions to the church, especially for the repayments to the Revolving Building Fund.

It is common in Japan for church members to be reluctant to change their membership even when they move to another district. But if they do, with the membership usually goes the offering.

Word got around that Mrs. Nakata was at last transferring her membership to a Sapporo church. It was soon realised by one rather unspiritual member that with the transfer of membership would go her monthly offering. But the missionaries, Mabel Fredlund and Jan Newsom, felt it right to ask the Lord to send them, as a gift to the Kutchan church building fund, a sum equivalent to what they were not receiving from Mrs. Nakata. They estimated that this would be 120,000 yen (US$400), but said nothing of it to the other church members, as they did not wish to foster an unhealthy and mercenary aspect of church membership.

Meanwhile, a gift had been received from a previous short-term missionary, 'to be used where most needed'. The Superintendent, after prayer and consultation with his Finance Committee, decided on its distribution.

He had no knowledge of the situation that had arisen in Kutchan when he said to the Committee, 'I would like to allocate 120,000 *yen* to the Kutchan church for their building fund, to help them repay their loan from the Revolving Fund'.

The delight of the elders of the church can be imagined when, a week later, the Superintendent drew out of his pocket twelve 10,000 *yen* notes and placed them before them. Their immediate reaction was to hasten the day when they would invite a Japanese pastor to minister to them. It is equally easy to imagine the secret delight of the two missionaries when they heard of the exact answer to their prayers.

To complete the picture, it should be said that as an added bonus to the church, Mrs. Nakata has not discontinued sending her contributions.

No two leaves on a tree are alike and, in the realm of God's providence, He seldom repeats His method of supply. Ruth Beckett had experience of this when on furlough.

'It was Christmas. My funds were all but exhausted. I was due to go to a camp on Boxing Day and needed money for travel and fees. On December 23rd two cheques arrived in the mail, but it would take at least a week, on account of the holiday, for the bank transactions to be made, before I could draw on them. How would the Lord meet my need? Christmas Eve brought a cheque from a friend in our suburb, to be drawn on her account which was in the very same bank as mine, and I was able to draw on it that very day!

'In March two of us made a deputation trip to the South Island by car. Funds in hand, I knew, were insufficient to cover the cost of the four-week journey. While writing a letter shortly before leaving, a line of a poem on the letter-head caught my eye: "The Lord will provide all that I need for my journey."

'So I set out, confident that the Lord would do as He had promised. As we totalled up our expenses at the end of the month, it was marvellous to see how, to the very cent, the money had been given as we travelled around, without our saying a word to anyone, which exactly covered the trip's expenses, even to the purchasing of new windscreen wipers for the OMF car!'

The kindly provision of a heavenly Father moved Elaine Mitchell, wife of the Field Director for Japan and Korea to share their experience with us.

Ruth Young carried the responsibility for catering for a large number of new workers who were studying Japanese in Sapporo. A larger kitchen and dining area than that in the building where they were housed was urgently needed.

As the Mitchells had formerly borne this responsibility, their house had been built with that factor in mind. It seemed only right that they should relinquish it in favour of the language students. On their return from furlough they had offered to do so, but the one responsible would not then hear of it. So now, everything was arranged for them to move to a smaller house next door.

Only two nights before the move was to be made, an invitation came to occupy the Mennonite Mission's hostel for children for a year. That night they could not sleep for thinking of all the advantages of God's unexpected provision.

Their eldest child, Christine, had finished at the OMF school and her parents were anticipating her attending the International School in Sapporo. If they had re-mained in their old neighbourhood, she would have had to travel by bus. But now they would be only a stone's throw away and she could walk to school. In addition, the provision of this new accommodation released the smaller house for two new workers who were arriving that month.

They relinquished a spacious home, and God gave them an ideal home for their large family.

While we all subscribe to the truth that 'in everything God works for good with those who love him, who are called according to his purpose',[1] there is a freshness in every new experience of God's kindly providence. It was certainly so with Dr. John Toop of Thailand.

'Have you ever wondered why the Lord allows you to do foolish little things? My wife was off to Bangkok for a literature committee meeting and forgot to tell Prajuab, our house girl, not to make bread; the girl started making it. I went off to the hospital; Prajuab did her chores and went home for breakfast.

'Usually she is away a couple of hours but, having left the bread to rise, she returned in half an hour to see to it. To her surprise the hasp of the lock was bent but the lock was still there. She went round to the back door (very rarely opened) and saw some of the small slats near the door jamb had been torn out and the door opened— and she heard steps, of someone moving about the room upstairs. Burglars!

'Terrified, Prajuab set off at a dead run across the eighty yards of field between us and the main road. Stopping an unknown cyclist who was headed into town, she asked him to tell the police that a thief was in the house. In short order two policemen arrived and entering the back door caught the thief unawares. Prajuab phoned her husband, who works in the hospital, and told me that the police wanted me to check our things.

'When I arrived, crowds of people were milling around to see the thief, a thin dejected youth of eighteen

[1] Romans 8.28.

named Chu Suk. He had made a pretty thorough search of our stuff and put some things into a bag. He was taken off to the police station and Prajuab and I had to go along and make statements.

'Two days later I had to go again and Chu Suk was there in his little cage, awaiting transfer to the provincial capital. I was able to see him and give him three tracts to read. Almost in tears, he asked me to forgive him and I said I did. He is now probably in the provincial gaol at Chainat with four others who recently robbed our nurse aides' residence.

'It was as if the Lord knew Satan was sending Chu Suk to burgle the house, and by letting Prajuab make the bread He ensured her returning unexpectedly. But is the Lord so concerned about our things? Was it not His desire that Chu Suk should get the Word of Life? Had Chu Suk been handed those identical tracts three days before, he would probably have glanced at them or even ridiculed them. As it was he received them when he had nothing else to read and was in a solemn state of mind. We gave thanks for the preservation of our belongings, but much more the spiritual welfare of Chu Suk was made our personal concern.'

One of the astonishing attributes of God is His humility. This is seen nowhere more clearly than in His individual interest in each of His creatures, down to the despised sparrow. To Him no one is unimportant and their affairs are His concern.

Annette Harris tells of meeting a Chinese boy from Sarawak while on furlough in England. His father died in August 1971, and since then he had taken over his father's business, had married, and was about to set up house in Pontianak, West Kalimantan, the town where

Annette works. He owns the timber concession that belonged to his father, and provides employment for many of the Christian refugees in that area, among whom she ministers. He has now found a spiritual home in the Chinese church in Pontianak.

'Before I left London,' she writes, 'an Indonesian boy began coming to the Gunnersbury Baptist Church that I attended. He told me that his father used to be an evangelist in Jakarta and conducted a weekly meeting in his home. About a year previously he collapsed while preaching and had since died. The meeting is still conducted by the boy's widowed mother.

'On my leaving, he requested me to take something to his little sister for her birthday. When I asked for the address, it turned out to be 'Jalan Kartini 1/7'. The address of the OMF Headquarters is Jalan Kartini 6/2 —the very same street in Jakarta, a city with a population of 5,000,000! I'm going to visit his mother this afternoon'.

As is often the case between cities, there is a friendly rivalry between Vancouver and Victoria in British Columbia. The apocryphal story is told by residents of Vancouver of a man who died one Sunday on the steps of the Post Office in Victoria. His body was discovered the next Tuesday morning!

But Edith Cork's experience at a Post Office in Malaysia would almost be in the same category.

One day, on returning home after a quick bicycle ride to post some letters, she found that her bag which she had put on her luggage-carrier was no longer there. In it was her purse containing, among other things, her driving licence and the precious identity card—a very important item in those days of emergency. What should she do? To ride back and look for it on a busy road would surely be useless. Report it to the police? Not very hopeful.

She decided to ride back, just to see. Imagine her surprise and joy to see her bag in the pathway and untouched, although scores of people had passed in and out of the Post Office in the intervening period. God had closed their eyes or restrained their cupidity, and protected her bag. Such visible evidence of an invisible God's personal interest and care brings Him very near.

This story from Norman Blake must bring this chapter to a conclusion.

For many years Norman has also been seconded by the OMF to the Far East Broadcasting Company in Manila, Philippines. Here he recounts how the Cheju Island Korean project of FEBC has been prospered by the Lord. The detailed answers to prayer indicate the hidden superintending providence of God.

Writing in 1972 he said: 'It may appear to some that progress on the Cheju project has been slow. But those of us who have been involved in the work have been aware of the hand of the Lord working for us on numerous occasions.

'The initial application to erect the broadcasting station was granted within six months, instead of a possible four years. The land on which it is to be erected is some of the best on the island. A sympathetic Governor's office obtained the land from more than sixty owners within six weeks! (How long would this take in our home countries?) And to crown all, the Lord provided an amount in the vicinity of US$70,000 so that the purchase price could be paid in cash when the deeds were signed.

'The provision of a good and honest contractor to

undertake construction has greatly facilitated the super-vision of all the buildings. Some farmers in New Zealand were apprised of the need of grass seed to sow down the area for pasture. They provided not only the grass seed, but also the necessary fertiliser and the costs of sowing.

'A tractor and implements were loaned for a number of months by the Isodor Ranch on the island and this has enabled the removal of hundreds of tons of rocks to the boundary fence. On one occasion, when power was cut off from our homes as the result of a typhoon, this same group loaned us a portable generator for six weeks, until FEBC could provide our own from special funds.

'The site has no water near by, so the schedule for drilling a well on our property was advanced by more than six months, only to discover that the rock base contained no water down to 150 feet. As it seemed hope-less, it was planned to quit boring. But prayer was made and the men drove a smaller drill to 210 feet. Then the water level came up to 80 feet! We now have all the water we need.'

The completion of the project was delayed for some months because the antennae and transmitter for the 250,000-watt station were held up by the Korean Customs authorities. But this equipment was later re-leased and the station is now 'on the air' to penetrate the whole of Communist China, as well as Japan, Korea and much of the USSR, loudly and clearly with the gospel.

'Omnipotence Hath Servants Everywhere'

PAUL assures us that it is one function of the Holy Spirit to impart to each believer that spiritual equipment that He sees will enable him to discharge the special form of service to which God calls him. 'All these (gifts) are inspired by one and the same Spirit, who apportions to each one individually as He wills.'[1] Not every believer knows what gifts, either of nature or of grace, may be latent in him, but God has His own method of bringing to light these unsuspected talents of His children.

Dr. Northcote Deck, leader of the South Sea Evangelical Mission in the Solomon Islands and for many years a member of the London Council of the CIM, told of his own experience. He maintained that the gift which God had blessed most richly in his ministry would never have come to light but for the exigencies of his missionary work.

Circumstances ordered by God led him to commence writing expositions of Scripture for the SSEM magazine. He discovered that he had a flair for writing articles that God was pleased to bless and use around the globe.

The same Lord led Linnet McIntosh into a totally unexpected and fruitful avenue of service, for which she had no idea that she possessed special gifts. But the remarkable way in which God confirmed His call to engage in this special ministry left her in no doubt of His purpose for her life.

[1] I Corinthians 12.11.

'The very first tithe from my own earnings,' she writes, 'was sent to the new Evangel Book Centre in Kuala Lumpur where my father had just started his new career as a literature worker. That was in 1956. A van for colportage work was needed, and it delighted me to know that my gift met a specific need.

'Nine years later, a very disappointed girl sat in the Overseas Director's office in Singapore. Her application for an Indonesian visa had finally been rejected after a wait of two long years.

'So now what? Mr. Lea was saying, "There is an urgent need for someone to go up-country to the Evangel Book Centre, as the manager has to go home for health reasons. We have considered the matter very carefully and feel that you are the right one to go. Another missionary from Malaysia has volunteered to go too, so you won't be alone. Of course we realise that neither of you has had any experience in this kind of work, but we believe that you can do it. After all, your father is an outstanding literature worker."

'I looked at him in shocked surprise. "Mr. Lea, I'm afraid you've got the wrong girl. I'm a school teacher and know absolutely nothing about business. Besides, I'm very sure I have not inherited my father's capabilities along this line."

' "Don't be too hasty," he replied. "I don't want your decision now. Please go away and pray about it."

'I left his office with the unspoken retort, "Yes, but one must be practical. If the Mission were to send me over to Manila for a month to the OMF Publishers, where I could follow my father around and ask all those naïve questions I would not dare ask anyone else, then perhaps we might have a talking point." For various reasons, however, I knew this would be quite out of the question.

'So I didn't even pray for such an opportunity. Neither, I confess, was I praying too seriously about that impossible proposition. But God was in this thing.

'One month later, Mr. Lea telephoned the school where I was temporarily teaching. He said, "Your mother has to go to hospital for surgery immediately. It is advisable that someone accompany her there. Seeing it is time for your annual leave we wonder if you would like to do this. It would be nice for her to have you, and also it would save us having to withdraw another missionary from her work. But I am sorry the Fellowship will not be able to help you financially. The whole trip would have to be at your own expense. Please let me know your decision today, as you will have to leave this week."

'I dropped that receiver as though it had been red-hot! With stunned certainty I knew that this was it, and that I was to go. The fact that my bank balance was totally inadequate hardly registered as a possible reason for refusal.

'Within a week I was flying to Manila, still trying to catch my breath. Most of my friends in Singapore were still unaware I had gone. The verse through which the Lord confirmed His leading for me to join the OMF came back to me with renewed meaning: "Behold, I have set the land before you; go in and take possession of the land which the Lord swore to your fathers . . . to give to them and to their descendants after them."[2] Was this command to be fulfilled quite as literally as this? Literature work? Evangel Book Centre?

'My mother's operation was successful. During her convalescence I learned a lot about the workings of a

[2] Deuteronomy 1.8.

Philippine hospital. This was a Christian hospital that stood in the middle of the notoriously wicked area of Tondo. Victims of stabbing or shootings were admitted daily.

'When my mother was well enough to be left I went to OMF Publishers. And there I followed my father around, asking all those naïve questions. The training was invaluable.

'During the month I was away from Singapore, I received a number of unexpected gifts of money. Most of them were quite small and came in the form of Singapore dollars and Philippine *pesos*. One lady in Singapore, when she heard of my sudden departure, gave me US$40 towards my fare. Someone else sent me an anonymous gift of US$30. And two unusually large personal donations arrived from friends in New Zealand who could not possibly have known of my particular need for funds.

'As I flew back to Singapore, I totted up all these gifts. The total figure was almost exactly US$232—my return air fare from Singapore to Manila!

'So the decision was made for me. Two weeks later I was standing in the Evangel Book Centre, a bewildered girl who had, however, an unshakable conviction that God had put her there. And so began seven years of the richest and most satisfactory missionary work that I could ever have imagined.

'Now, in 1972, I stand again on the threshold of Indonesia. But this time I am going in joyfully as a literature worker, to face greater challenges than ever before, for which all the experience of the past years has been an essential preparation.

'If that young student teacher, who sent her first tithe to the Evangel Book Centre in 1956 could have seen the years ahead, she would have been amazed. Certainly

it is a wonderful thing to have one's life planned by
God.'

'Had I known what He was keeping for me,' wrote
Samuel Rutherford, 'I should never have been so faint-
hearted.'

When God bestows special gifts on His servants, He is
concerned to see that they find employment in His service, and is pleased to intervene in unostentatious yet
remarkable ways to make this possible.

Since instrumental music has always occupied so large
a place in the worship and service of the Church, we
should not be surprised that God is concerned about the
praise of His people. Some of our missionaries have experienced His providential leading in obtaining musical
instruments that would make the praise of the Church
more tuneful, and contribute more effectively to the
worship of the Church.

Alice Compain, a gifted violinist, has employed her
talent in gospel radio ministry in both Thailand and
Laos, and is now in Cambodia. At the request of the
Lao National Radio, she recorded some Lao national
songs to the accompaniment of violin and organ.

'When I went home on furlough in 1963,' she writes,
'my violin looked crooked and was difficult to play on.
It had come unstuck twice, and the second time a Viet-
namese carpenter had done his best to make it useable,
but the strings were too high above the finger-board.
When I reached London, I went to the shop from which
I had purchased the violin fifteen years previously for
£30. They examined it and were very sympathetic,
but told me the violin would have to be taken completely apart and the cost of repairs would be £40. I
accepted their recommendation to think things over!

'In the course of my first week at home, I met one

of my prayer companions who had been for many years a secretary at the OMF, Newington Green. As she was a keen amateur player herself, she naturally inquired about my violin. She suggested that I take it to an amateur violin maker whom she knew. In his spare time he made violins in a small tool-house in his garden, and also led a small orchestra.

'He undertook the job, saying it would not be ready for three months, but gave no indication of the cost. I was sure, however, the Lord had guided so far, and when I collected a straight-looking violin all re-glued, he asked only for the cost of the materials, £5.60.

'When thanking him, I explained how God had worked out His purposes in my life. I was delighted to see this man, not yet a Christian, attending my vale-dictory service, before I returned to Laos with a good violin!'

The guitar has won an honourable place in the con-temporary music of our youth and no less so among the young people of Asia. In addition to being a very portable instrument on the missionfield, its music is much appreciated by most races.

When on furlough in Australia in 1970, Daphne Roberts very much wanted a guitar for use in her Scripture Union work when she returned to Malaysia. Some young teachers got to hear of this through a mutual friend and laid their plans.

'On four successive days I received cheques for $15, marked "for a guitar". I was overwhelmed by their love, as they had met me only that year. When I went to buy the guitar, I found a very good one which was reduced in price, as the maker was producing a new line. This meant that I could buy teaching books and other extras as well.

'I returned to Malaysia with a guitar that wins admiration from all who hear it. It has of course been a great help in my Scripture Union work.'

Surprised by Joy is the title of a notable autobiography, but it was also the experience of Helen Anderson.

When she graduated from college in the USA, her parents toyed with the idea of presenting her with a piano, but financial and other reasons decided them against it. 'In my own heart I knew a secret reason,' she writes. 'God was calling me to the mission field and I would have to leave the piano behind. Later, a relative who had been in China as a missionary said that there was a piano in Shanghai that I could have. But when I arrived in China in 1934, I discovered that it was not available.

'When I went to the Language School, a piano seemed further away than ever, except when we paid a visit to the compound of another Mission. The realisation swept over me that in the days to come, not only would their be no opportunities to play the piano, but also I would probably lose any ability I had to play.

'The years passed with only occasional opportunities for piano music both for my musically talented husband and myself, at some conference or while on furlough. I never had any real sense of sacrifice, for that was unlikely in the joyful, satisfying service of Him who had given me His all.

'After coming to Yü Shan Theological Institute in Taiwan in 1971, I discovered that these tribal students were very musical. With such potentialities for musical expression of praise to the Lord, I began to yearn desperately for a piano of our own, on which we could work and help them in their harmony training.

'An urge to "ask", with the subsequent "you will receive",[3] gripped me, but I was assailed with doubts. "You are too old now." "You don't know how long you will be here." But the urge to ask continued, as did the doubts, until one day I said, "Lord, I know you can give us a piano. But if we were to obtain one, I would want a new one with all expenses paid in such a clear way that I would have no qualms of conscience in having it."

'A week or two later I received a letter from a friend whom I have seen only three or four times in thirty-eight years, and from whom I hear only about three times a year. Another letter came from her the next week which she trusted would "come as a special blessing from the Lord." She said that she had asked for a word from the Lord to confirm the strong urge from within and He had given it. In the letter was $500, "to be used in a personal way for yourself". This I knew was the Lord's answer. A wave of conviction of the sin of my unbelief came over me. How does one thank Him for such a gift? And for the giver?

'In years gone by we would have questioned the rightness of having a piano in the area where we lived. But the economic growth in this country has brought many pianos from Japan and some are being made locally. I pray that only music for His glory will come from my piano. We can never overtake His giving.'

The spread of the gospel and the growth of the Church in mission lands must become the burden, not of the western missionary alone, but of the national Christians themselves. Indigenous spiritual movements with a basis of practical faith therefore became a matter of special concern. It is consequently a great encouragement to

[3] Matthew 21.22.

the missionary when national Christians to whom they
have ministered display a growing spiritual maturity, for
it is they who will mould the church of the future.

A Chinese Christian lady expressed her vital interest
in the work of the OMF by bringing several substantial
monetary gifts to the office in Bangkok, Thailand. It
was always in cash, and always with the request that it
be treated as anonymous. One large gift came at a time
of crisis in the medical work of the Mission.

In 1969 the need of a higher-level evangelical Bible
College for the training of Thai pastors and Christian
workers was becoming increasingly felt. The OMF had
established a Bible School at Phayao in North Thailand,
but it was geared to the training of laymen who had
been denied the advantage of higher education.

This same lady had previously provided the funds for
the Chinese-speaking Bethel Bible School in Bangkok.
She offered the OMF a block of land adjoining this
Bible School, on which to build such a higher-level
college. After prayer and investigation, however, the
Mission leaders did not discern the hand of God in the
proposal.

It was a strong conviction of the Thailand Superintendent, Cyril Faulkner, that the need was for a Thai
Bible College using only the Thai language, but also
teaching English to a standard that would enable them
to have access to the wealth of English biblical literature that is available.

It seemed like turning down a wonderful offer. But
the negotiating missionaries prayed with the lady and
her family. Then the three donors went aside for private
consultation. In a few minutes they were back with
another offer: 'We will give you 500,000 *baht*
(US$25,000) which is the value of the land—and there

may be more to follow. So you can build the college wherever you see best.'

In co-operation with the Christian and Missionary Alliance, the OMF has now erected the Bangkok Bible College, and a promising group of well qualified Thai students are now in training for God's work in their own land.

In more recent years, greater stress has rightly been laid on the desirability of missionaries taking some special studies or refresher courses while at home on furlough. Sometimes extra leave is granted to give time to enable the missionary to gain better equipment for the term ahead.

God's plan for Daphne Roberts in ways other than financial, in the area of extra studies, proved to her the reality of a heavenly Father's care.

'In 1964 I returned to Australia with the OMF's blessing, to finish my Arts course which I had begun before I went overseas. I hoped, too, to do my Diploma of Education. This meant two years of intensive study following a course which, I realised later, would have been almost impossibly demanding.

'Soon after reaching home, I met a friend who told me that the Bachelor of Education had been made a primary degree specially for trained teachers. Through her help the university allowed me to transfer my previously acquired Arts subjects to the B.Ed. course.

'Normally the degree is granted only to practising teachers, which I was not. However, when I explained that my work in Malaysia involved training young people, the Dean of the Faculty pleaded my case with the Professor and permission was given for me to receive the degree if I passed the examinations.

'This meant that I had to do only two subjects in

1964, and these could be taken part-time, thus leaving me time for some deputation work. This left three full subjects for 1965, a much more reasonable course than I had expected to take. The degree I received has proved much more helpful in my special work than the Arts degree would have been.

'During that year God supplied my financial needs in many ways. Owing to the death of my father, money was available for my university fees, and the light study programme meant smaller expenses.

'In 1964 I was receiving the usual OMF allowance, but in 1965 I was on leave of absence, truly on faith. What a remarkable year it was! Gifts came from many unexpected sources, sometimes from people whom I had not seen for years. Twice I received anonymous gifts of $100 and to this day I have no idea from whom they came. I kept a record of all I received and was astounded at the total. Truly a thrilling year.'

It is now almost twenty years since work was opened up in two coastal towns of West Kalimantan, Indonesia. Two of those who pioneered the work among the Chinese residents were Robert and Martha Peterson of Portland, Oregon.

As the work developed and the church grew in maturity, God's servants were burdened to pray for the establishment of a Bible School. In due time the project which bore the marks of being born of God became a reality. On September 23rd, 1971, in Singkawang, the *Word of the Lord Bible Institute* came to birth.

'At the dedication service, we sat in wonder as we heard of God's miracles,' Bob reported. Premises sought and needed were purchased at an incredibly low price. At each stage of the project the needed funds were provided. Government permission and recognition were granted. This was a miracle indeed in Indonesia, considering the red tape involed!

'Sufficient faculty members came in answer to prayer, five in all, and more are promised for next year. Yet of what use are premises and faculty without students? God sent us exactly what we requested. Five men and seven women students enrolled for the first year. All seem to show promise and a personal call from God.'

Projects born of God and sustained by prayer achieve great things for God.

Two candidates for work with the OMF in Japan were faced with an acute dilemma—an outfit list for Singapore and Japan, and no money.

'I had just finished Bible College,' testified Mariana Nesbit, 'and Jim had two more terms to go. My salary for part-time teaching was well used to pay for current living expenses and to pay off a debt caused by a burglary. How were we going to buy cotton clothes and, even worse, such un-South African items as snow-boots, heavy overcoats, warm woollen clothing and fleecy-lined underwear?

'The months passed. We priced what we could find in Cape Town and were appalled. No extra money for outfit was received and I worried myself sick. What were we going to do? I did not even know what a dress that would be suitable for temperatures below zero centigrade would look like.

'I tried to trust the Lord, but felt very hopeless. At one Sunday service we attended, the reading was from Matthew 6.30 "... will he not much more clothe you, O men of little faith?"

'Faith lifted a little, but it took a second reading of this passage at another church service shortly after to encourage me to really believe that God would provide.

Faith rested in assurance, and soon the flood of provision started. One day the provision was so overwhelming that I actually asked God to stop spoiling us!

'Friends sent small gifts in cash. Some gave articles of clothing, not knowing that they supplied exact needs. One woman of slight acquaintance, from our church, took us shopping. We were supplied with the best quality garments we have ever owned.

'A number of garments were left at the OMF Mission Home for missionaries to select as they chose. My employer's wife had died some time previously, and he invited me to select anything I wanted.

'When we left South Africa, our hearts were full of gratitude and joy and our packing cases filled to the brim with high-quality clothes suitable for Sapporo and six feet of snow.

". . . will he not much more clothe you, O men of little faith?" '

One final experience which does not occur very often came as a tremendously heartening experience to God's sometimes hard pressed children.

The Director of Finance and Administration was reporting in 1972 on an 'over and above' provision, over and above what we asked.

'The Lord surprised us with unusually generous funds for the second quarter of this year. To our great joy He sent, from all sources, a total of US$368,472 (almost £148,000); 135 per cent of the amount we were praying for. Praise the Lord! That this was His doing is shown by the amounts received at six of our home centres: Germany, 108 per cent;[4] New Zealand, 150 per cent; Singapore and Malaysia, 190 per cent; Switzerland, 362 per cent; UK, 113 per cent; and USA, 204 per

[4] i.e. percentage of the amount each country was praying for.

cent. As a result, some long outstanding needs have been met.'

> 'I know how to be abased, and I know how to abound . . . I have learned the secret of facing . . . abundance and want.'[5]

[5] Philippians 4.12.

A Mosaic of His Faithfulness

What shall I do when the brook runs dry,
  And the ravens come no more?
Thy Father God, who reigns on high,
  Thy utmost need can still supply
From His exhaustless store.

F. Houghton

It must have been a severe test of Elijah's faith to sit
and watch the Cherith stream, on which he depended
for his water supply, slowly drying up. But he learned
there many lessons in the school of faith, for the failing
water afforded God an excellent opportunity to display
His resourcefulness. The testing prepared the way for
the memorable experience of the unwasting meal and
the unfailing oil.

There are few callings in life that hold more possibilities of testing and trial than that of the missionary
and, be it also said, of tremendous compensations. From
the experiences of a number of missionaries we will
construct a mosaic of His faithfulness.

Someone has written that 'He who had nowhere to
lay His head, rarely allows His followers to be so placed'.
But there are exceptions even to this. To those who are
unfamiliar with the problems of missionaries, especially
single ladies when they go home on furlough, it may
seem extravagant to say that it sometimes can be a
traumatic experience.

Home circumstances, accommodation, loneliness, and

culture-shock in reverse can all compound the problem. But in this realm as in every other, 'those who trust Him wholly, find Him wholly true'. The experience of one lady missionary will demonstrate how God provided the solution for this very real problem.

For this lady going home on furlough, there were secret fears and misgivings. Many changes had taken place. The old home had gone. There would be neither father nor mother to welcome her. The home she had loved so much had been sold.

But God had been working and He had provided another lovely home—just the kind of place she loved. A dear friend had built herself a bungalow in the old home town, and the upstairs room was to be hers. Such a cosy room it was, with a window alcove where her boxes made a window seat. Furniture from her own home had been installed—her father's table, mother's chair, and her own chest of drawers. There were built-in cupboards for storing things. A wash-basin fitted into another alcove. What an ideal room for a missionary on furlough!

And there was a lovely garden, and a Christian friend with whom she could have fellowship. Yes, she had lost her home, but God had proved true to His promise: 'Truly, I say to you, there is no man who has left house or wife or brothers or parents or children, for the sake of the kingdom of God, who will not receive manifold more in this time, and in the age to come eternal life'.[1] But this was not all. Another furlough provision was for holidays. Her married sister had a cottage by the sea, and she could spend as long as she liked in that lovely seaside town, and enjoy holidays such as she herself could never have afforded.

Another of God's provisions was for clothes. Summer

[1] Luke 18.29, 30.

sales were on and it was fun to walk down Oxford Street and Regent Street, looking in the windows to see what she would buy. But it was 'only pretend' because she did not then have the money to buy such things.

But her heavenly Father had been planning for her. The very next post brought a letter with a cheque for £10 enclosed. It was from a Christian lady who had never sent in this way before or since.

The missionary knew what the money was meant for! That very day she had a shopping spree, retracing her steps of the evening before and actually buying the shoes and other things she had seen and wanted.

In these mechanised days, a car is more or less a necessity for the missionary on furlough who desires to engage in deputation work. Not all missionaries are in a position to purchase one, but God delights to be trusted to supply every genuine need of His children.

When she arrived home for furlough in England in 1970 Edith Cork longed for a small car. It would enable her to visit friends while engaged in deputation work, and also to take aged relatives for outings. However, she never had sufficient money to buy a car, nor indeed for more than her needs from day to day.

A few days after she reached home, a friend asked her, 'Would you like a car for your furlough?' Then came the offer. 'I will advance you the money to purchase a second-hand car for your use during furlough. Then it can be sold when you return, and the money repaid to me. She bought the car and sold it when she returned to Malaysia for only £5 less than she had paid for it. In addition, all running costs were met. So her heavenly Father provided her with a car for her whole furlough at a cost to her of only £5!

Return to the 'field' held for her another faith-confirming proof of a loving Father's interest.

One day a gift of £5 unexpectedly arrived from England. 'Two days later,' she wrote, 'a Chinese friend came to visit us, so we drove to Fraser's Hill tourist resort. On arrival, my glasses fell into my lap. The frames had collapsed. Fortunately I can see well, long distance, so driving home was no problem. But teaching in the Christian Training Centre was impossible.

'Although the gift was insufficient to pay for new bifocal spectacles, it enabled me to go to the optician and have my eyes tested. Next day I had a rest at 1.15 p.m. and rose again at 2 p.m. On going to my desk, I found an envelope with a pair of glasses drawn on the front, indicating that the enclosed M$50 was the answer to my prayer! Now I had a little more than was needed. But God's accounting is never wrong, for within a few days my car had to be repaired, so that need was met too.'

To the missionary in the United States, the prospect of major surgery is far from comfortable from a financial point of view. How was the heavy cost of hospital and operation to be met?

With her husband she was invited for deputation ministry to a town they had never visited. They found themselves in the hospitable home of a lovely Christian family. Two adorable young children of two and three years met them at the door. They became good friends, even at the dinner table.

Later on, as she helped the mother with the dishes in the kitchen, varied subjects were discussed, including the anticipated hospital visit. The charming little children were there too. Then her hostess said, 'We are so thankful you love our children. We have wanted them to

grow up loving missionaries, but we were almost afraid
to have you come. The last missionary we had completely ignored the small girls, and I was afraid they
would never want another missionary'.

'After that happy weekend,' the missionary wrote,
'the mother and the wee tots asked that we kneel at the
bedside and pray together.

'We returned to Philadelphia. About five days before
the hospital visit, we received from these friends a
cheque for $500, designated for my medical expenses.'

One day, early in 1962, a big fair-haired member of
the Fellowship walked into the office of the Treasurer at
Singapore and said as he handed in his accounts, 'Fred,
from the look of these accounts you will think that either
I have juggled them or that there is something providential in them!'

He had just returned from six months' itinerant
ministry among the Chinese churches in Singapore and
Malaya, during which he had, as his custom was, kept
a careful and detailed account of his expenses. Forty-
three separate items ranged from ten-cent bus fares to
$20.00 railway tickets. When he totalled them all up,
they amounted to $103.01.

There was nothing surprising in that. The surprising
thing was the other account he had kept—the record of
unexpected, unsolicited honoraria that had been handed
to him by many of the Chinese churches in which he
had been ministering. He had accepted them gratefully,
not because they supplied any pressing need, but because,
like Paul, he rejoiced that there should be fruit to their
account.[2]

But when he realised that, added together, those gifts
totalled exactly $103.00, only one cent less than his

[2] cf. Philippians 4.17.

expenses account, he felt strangely humbled. He knew he could not attribute this experience to mere coincidence. Coming as it did at a critical juncture in his missionary career, it seemed as though the Father's hand had gripped his arm, confirming His personal interest in the affairs of His child.

One of the great encouragements to the medical missionary is when some patient not only responds to treatment, but presses on to become a valuable propagator of the gospel. Mrs. Samang of North-east Thailand became sick. Telling of her case, Dr. June Morgan wrote :

'Fifteen years is a long time. A long time to have frequent fevers, running sores, nose-bleeds and painful nerves. Leprosy is a nasty disease, and Mrs. Samang had it in its most unpleasant form.

'After years of treatment at home, she came to the OMF Hospital at Manorom. She did not respond well to the treatment, and on several occasions she nearly died.

'Knowing her love for the Lord and her desire to be with Him prompted us to pray several times that He might take her to Himself, where she would be free from her suffering. But He had other and better plans for her.

'In 1967 a Swiss pharmaceutical firm offered the hospital free drugs for use for problem patients, on an experimental basis. Mrs. Samang was not one chosen to go on trial. After a few months of using these drugs, however, their value was so obvious that we asked the firm if we could give her some. The answer was, Yes.

'After a few weeks she stopped having fevers. There were no further nose-bleeds or aching nerves, and her skin cleared. For the first time in years she began to feel well and was able to attend the whole of the Leprosy

Church Conference. Previously she had been able to attend for one day at the most.

'The following year she organised and supervised all the catering arrangements for the Conference—no small task when over two hundred people attend the meetings.

'She later entered Bible School to prepare for further years of Christian usefulness. We praise God for her recovery, and for that of the other one hundred or so other patients who have been restored to health through the use of this drug'.

Towards the end of 1973 Mrs. Samang was married to Mr. Saweng, who worked at the Manorom Hospital for many years, and together they are serving the Lord.

For a number of years Helen Bosshardt had been interested in the OMF, but was not certain that God was calling her to serve under its banner. At the English Keswick in 1971, however, she clearly heard God's call.

'When I returned to St. Chrischona Bible School in Switzerland, I faced a very difficult family situation, and did not feel that I could tell my parents at that time of my call to OMF. Weeks passed by and doubts began to assail me.

'I was planning to attend the OMF Conference and had been led to pray that, if the Lord really wanted me to apply to that Mission, He would impress one of the leaders to ask me about my plans for the future.

'Before the conference commenced, Mr. Stäheli, the Swiss Home Director, approached me with the news that a lady in Germany wished to provide money for a SPOT[3] short-term worker to go to Thailand. I had not heard of the SPOT programme, and I told him that I wasn't particularly interested in Thailand, but I was definitely interested in the Philippines.

[3] Summer Programme for Overseas Training.

'He contacted the donor. Not only was she willing for the change of field, but she offered to pay the extra $250 involved in travel.

'I asked Mr. Stäheli why he had approached me. He said that the Holy Spirit had clearly impressed him to do so. He had felt for some time that I was interested in the OMF, although I had made no approach.

'Apart from this financial provision, I would have been unable to go, and through this experience I now know that the Lord would have me apply to the OMF for long-term service.'

The divine mathematics match the divine love.

Denis Lane, Overseas Director of the OMF, was booked to make a tour of the United States in 1972 on the business of the Fellowship. Whether he should travel alone or his wife June should accompany him depended on the Lord's direct provision. 'So we asked Him to supply the necessary US$1,353 Himself.'

'One friend sent £100 from a legacy. Two gifts of US$50 came. Another legacy brought it to US$564 just before Christmas. Imagine our joy when other friends who were planning a journey to East Asia, decided against it and sent £300 to us instead. But there was still US$88 outstanding! God knew, and we soon learned that non-residents can get reductions in the United States. This meant that we had sufficient for the full fare. God does provide!'

Tales From the Mails

IT might be inferred from stories of dramatic interventions of God, in sending large sums of money in time of special need, that the Mission is interested only in large gifts. This is by no means the case. Actually the greater part of Mission income is derived from the comparatively small gifts of a large body of faithful praying friends.

In proof of this is the fact that in 1972 more than 11,600 separate donations were received and individually acknowledged at our London headquarters alone. Many of these gifts were the outcome of a distinct spiritual impulse, the work of the Holy Spirit moving in an obedient heart. To this host of faithful friends any success in the work is in large measure due.

To the Mission officers who open the mail, it is often a romance rather than a chore, as they see the gift matching the urgent need, or as they are moved by reading of the heart-exercise and sacrifice lying behind some of the small donations.

Norman Pateman tells of a wonderful climax to the drama of the long drawn out British postal strike in 1971 that paralysed communications throughout the land. It is a novel thought that God can be glorified in a crippling strike, and yet it is true. We have come to regard these interruptions to normal business life as the almost inevitable outcome of the bitter hostility existing between capital and labour. But in this case the dark cloud had a silver lining.

In the British postal strike the heavenly Father's pre-vision was matched by His abundant provision.

In the two days before the strike began, gifts amounting to over £20,000, the equivalent of a normal month's receipts, were received at the London office of the OMF.

Included in this amount were two legacies that could easily have come earlier, or very much later. The timing of their arrival was highly significant. No less remarkable was the receipt, despite there being no postal deliveries, of about £6,000 within three days of the beginning of February.

During the strike, friends brought gifts themselves, or telephoned enquiring how to send gifts through the bank. One enthusiast even placed a cheque between two large sheets of hardboard and sent the parcel by British Rail!

At the beginning of March, a Bank Trust Company wrote the Secretary to say that they had been empowered under the will of a certain lady, who was unknown to Mission officers, to distribute the residue of her estate. They asked for a copy of the Mission's last statement of Accounts and Annual Report.

It later transpired that the Bank had received no fewer than three hundred letters from different charitable organisations soliciting help. (The OMF was not among them!) The Bank therefore asked the Director of the National Council of Social Service to make suggestions for the distribution of the residue of the estate. They adopted his recommendations, and among them the name of OMF appeared.

The result? A cheque for no less than £10,000 for our General Fund.

'At the same time,' concluded Mr. Pateman, 'a donor sent us a gift of a similar amount to enable special projects to be undertaken in East Asia.

'It was a very wonderful experience. Receipts in

London, for January to April 1971, during which the long strike occurred, actually exceeded those for the same period in 1970 by £8,345.'

No good will He withhold,
No evil can befall,
O faithless heart, be bold
To count on Him for all!

Though every road were barred,
Traffic with heaven is free,
And under angel guard
God's posts speed down to thee!
F. Houghton

A glimpse into the daily mail-bag, although not so spectacular as the above incident, pays its own tribute to the faithfulness of God, and the generosity of His obedient stewards.

An anonymous gift of £1,000 was accompanied by a little note : 'I have been very much exercised about this money which has been lying in my bank account, and I feel the Lord would have me send it to you.'

Two days later, another £1,000 arrived with just the simple comment at the end of the letter : 'I had some money unexpectedly, recently, and feel the enclosed should come to the OMF.'

And another : 'The morning after our OMF prayer meeting when I learned that £800 was required for the support of one missionary for a year, I heard from my solicitor that a mortgage was being redeemed. The mortgage was for £800, and I suddenly thought that perhaps the Lord would have me send the money to the OMF, so I am sending the cheque.'

An anonymous donor in Edinburgh sent a generous

gift with the following note : 'If the missionaries are taking a cut in allowance this quarter, I wish to share with them, and so am taking a similar cut from my salary this month—that they may not lack what I have received.'

'I have received an unexpected legacy, and should like the OMF to share it.' Enclosed in this brief letter was a cheque for £100.

A letter from the Christian Union of one of our universities brought £4.20 for medical work. The special interest of the gift was that it was the outcome of the students missing one lunch a week during Lent. But not only that, they had spent the hungry lunch hour praying for the work of the OMF.

Another gift was received from a clergyman who had known very little of ill-health during his life, but earlier in the year had become seriously ill. While he was incapacitated, someone had given him a copy of Bishop Houghton's book, *The Fire Burns On.*

'This spoke to my soul as has no other book for many years,' he wrote. 'As I read it and shed tears of penitence at the shallowness of my own life and ministry, spiritual healing came.'

Around the time this friend was reading the book, our heavenly Father was taking its author, a former General Director of the Mission to join the saints triumphant.

The Mission officers were engaged in a search for a hostel to accommodate quite a number of children of missionaries who were returning from overseas to continue their education in the homeland. A letter was received containing £2,500—the amount of the needed deposit on the new premises. With the cheque came the following letter :

'About 1931 I sent the China Inland Mission the sum

of £2. 10s. 0d., my tithe on the first commission of £25 I had ever earned. So, having now sold some holdings, I thought it would be fun to send £2,500 to the OMF as a token of the thousand-fold which the Lord has given me over the past forty years.'

A lady had set aside the sum of £1,000 to buy a car and help pay the running expenses. She decided, however, to make it a gift to the OMF. On the very day she despatched the cheque, a member of her family wrote saying that he would like to make her a gift of £1,000, and a cheque for the first half was enclosed in his letter.

Another gift of £1,000 was made possible by the sale of a property at a greatly enhanced price. It was sent because the vendor 'wished OMF and God's work in East Asia to share in the benefit'.

A touching gift of £5 towards the cost of the Manorom Christian Hospital, Thailand, came from eleven boys and girls aged eight to fifteen, patients at the Nuffield Orthopaedic Centre, who reported that they were 'getting better'.

Gifts from pensioners are always humbling. From their Christmas bonus of £10, the Mission received gifts of £1; £2.50, and £10; one of ten gifts to various societies; one of £5 to share with a worker in Laos. Accompanying the last gift was a note saying, 'Thankful for the Welfare State to care for us'.

An elderly friend sent £100 with the comment, 'I have lately had a gratuity on retiring and would wish to offer the Lord His share for His work.'

Another precious gift was for £3.50. The covering letter said, 'We are sorry that the amount has been smaller this year, but we have had no income for the last two years to tithe, so it has been rather difficult. We hope this will help a little.'

A note accompanying a cheque for £65.19 read, 'It is good to be able to send you the first fruits of a pay increase.'

Just after Christmas, a letter was received from a student, enclosing £20.35—'All the cash I received for Christmas presents'.

Money does not usually fall from heaven. It normally comes from warm human hearts and often at great sacrifice to the donor.

The element of sacrifice behind a gift to God's work imparts to it a peculiar potency. The fact that Mary could have kept her fragrant and valuable jar of anointing oil to enhance her own attractiveness made it especially precious to her Lord, and caused its fragrant ministry to pervade the world for two millenniums. So is it with the sacrificial gifts of God's children.

The continuing story of a pensioner in Christchurch, New Zealand, who was over ninety years of age, is an illustration of this fact. Here it is :

'I am sorry that it is quite a long time since I was able to send anything for Miss X. I had to buy a pair of shoes, and that meant $10 less for evangelism. I pray that others will supply my deficiency.'

Four months later she wrote, 'I have great pleasure in sending $4. I had my 90th birthday last month.' A month later : 'I am sending $6 for Miss X, $2 extra from my pension rise.'

A little later : 'Here is an extra $3 for Miss X, and I must tell you how I got it. You will be as amused as I am ! Since I have been in this home, friends have given me toilet soap, talcum powder, chocolates, biscuits, etc. Being on a diet, I can't eat the latter and have more than I need of the former. So with Christmas near, I decided to sell most of what I had and to send you part of the proceeds. Women who can't get out were glad to buy, and I am delighted to be able to give a little more to spread the good news in Asia.'

Gifts continued to come regularly. In March 1971 she wrote : 'I am delighted to be able to send $3 for Miss X —earned by making soft toys—at 94 years. We have many grannies here, and some have asked me to make soft toys for their grand- and great grand-children.'

Undaunted by rising costs she wrote in May : 'I am glad to be able to send $2 for Miss X. As our board goes up, my income goes down. I now pay more than twice as much as when I first came here, which means that much less for God's service.'

A few days later she wrote : 'The receipt for my $2 came today, and a few hours later another resident handed me $2, "for your mission". This is the first time anyone has done so and I am delighted to pass it on.' Again in September she forwarded another $5 someone had given her.

In August 1972 she wrote, 'I have just received the increase in the universal pension, and am thankful to be able to send $10 for Miss X. At 96 I wonder how long I will be able to continue sending help to you!'

This elect lady was of close kin to David who said, 'I will not offer burnt offerings to the Lord my God which cost me nothing'. Can you not sense the fragrance of such gifts?

'The Same For Ever'

THE stories told or retold in this slim volume range over more than a century. A century during which we have moved from horse buggy to moon buggy. A century that has accumulated more knowledge than all other centuries rolled together. A century in which kaleidoscopic change in every realm is accepted as the norm. Only God has not changed—and His faithfulness endures to all generations.

'Of old thou didst lay the foundation of the earth, and the heavens are the work of thy hands.

'They will perish, but thou dost endure; they will all wear out like a garment. Thou changest them like raiment and they pass away.

'*But thou art the same*, and thy years have no end.'[1]

The experiences of the divine faithfulness at the beginning of the century are here seen to be matched by those at the end. Trusting hearts in the nineteen-seventies are finding their God just as competent and worthy of their wholehearted confidence as did their counterparts in the 1870s. To use an old expression, God is our eternal Contemporary.

He is never taken by surprise, and never needs to resort to emergency action. He always knows what He will do, and He always responds to the trust reposed in Him. None who have relied on Him for needs great or small have ever found their trust betrayed.

[1] Psalm 102.25–27.

O make but trial of His love,
Experience will decide
How blest they are, and only they,
Who in His truth confide.

Appendix

A BRIEF HISTORY OF THE OVERSEAS
MISSIONARY FELLOWSHIP

THE China Inland Mission, founded in 1865 by James Hudson Taylor, had as its aim the evangelisation of all the inland provinces of the Chinese Empire. He had already worked for several years as a missionary in the coastal provinces, but broken health compelled him to return to England. It was only after months of deep inward conflict that he finally obeyed the divine urge to found a missionary society to achieve this God-given objective.

Within a year he went on his way to China, accompanied by his family and sixteen missionary recruits. The story of their early struggles and testings is graphically told in *The Biography of James Hudson Taylor* (OMF BOOKS). They were entirely without guaranteed financial support, but were quietly confident that God would supply their need. Nor was their trust in Him betrayed.

In spite of initial setbacks, the work prospered and grew until in 1937 it reached a peak membership of 1,387. This number included missionaries from a number of Associate Missions from Europe.

In 1951 Communist pressures compelled all missionaries to withdraw from China. However, the Mission leaders did not accept this as marking the end of the missionary contribution of the CIM. They were given satisfying guidance to re-deploy their workers in a number of countries in East Asia. The cumbersome name of the re-constituted Mission combined the old and the new: *China Inland Mission OVERSEAS MISSIONARY Fellowship (CIM-OMF)*.

In 1965, the centenary of the Mission, the name became simply *Overseas Missionary Fellowship*. At the time of writing, membership of the OMF stands at about 850. These missionaries are deployed in Japan, Korea, Taiwan, Hong Kong, the Philippines, Indonesia, Singapore, Malaysia, Thailand, Laos, South Vietnam and the Khmer Republic (Cambodia).

Members are drawn from many denominations, and from many countries—the United Kingdom, USA, Canada, Switzerland, Germany, Holland, South Africa, Australia, New Zealand, Japan, the Philippines, Hong Kong, Singapore and Malaysia. Home councils and home centres are in operation in most of these countries.